NOTES ON THE GERMAN PREPARATIONS FOR INVASION OF THE UNITED KINGDOM

(2nd Edition)

Published by
The Naval & Military Press Ltd
Unit 10, Ridgewood Industrial Park,
Uckfield, East Sussex,
TN22 5QE England
Tel: +44 (0) 1825 749494
Fax: +44 (0) 1825 765701

www.naval-military-press.com

Reproduced by kind permission of the Central Library,
Royal Military Academy, Sandhurst

COPY NO.

760

NOTES ON GERMAN PREPARATIONS FOR INVASION OF THE UNITED KINGDOM

(2nd Edition)

Prepared by the General Staff, War Office

M.I. 14,
January, 1942

[Security B 540]

CONTENTS

PART I

PART II

PART III

---

* *See* para. 4.

PART IV

Exercises and Special Weapons.

* *See* para. 4.

PART V

* *See* para. 4.

PART VI

LIMITING FACTORS.

PART VII

CHOICE OF TIME AND PLACE.

PART VIII

APPENDICES

* *See* para. 4.

* *See* para. 4.

APPENDICES

Appendices which are in the form of drawings, diagrams, maps, etc., are grouped together at the end of the book, viz. :—

(9372)

SECRET

PART I

INTRODUCTION

Purpose and Scope of Notes.

1. These Notes have been compiled with the assistance of the Admiralty and Air Ministry, and are intended to be a " vade mecum " of the military intelligence which bears directly on a possible attempt to invade the U.K., Northern Ireland and Eire; within this category must be included certain islands or groups of islands, *viz.*, the Shetlands, the Faroes and Iceland (C), which might form the object of subsidiary operations before or during the main operations.

2. Much information contained herein has already been circulated, but this summary, together with the information in the appendices, may be of assistance to commanders and staffs of formations.

3. The wider aspects of possible enemy strategy and tactics against the U.K. will only be referred to in so far as intelligence regarding the enemy, his methods and preparations, points specifically to particular possibilities.

Many considerations will influence the enemy's decision as to when and with what force to attempt an attack upon this country.

*4. In order that the Notes may be used as a Handbook for permanent reference and be kept up to date, the book is published in loose-leaf form and statistical and similar matter which is liable to amendment has been included in appendices.

So much additional information has become available since the original publication of these Notes in April, 1941, that the present edition has been entirely reprinted, and supersedes the former edition.

To facilitate reference, paragraphs and appendices which contain amendments of importance or information not published in the earlier edition are marked with an asterisk both in the text and in the Table of Contents.

PART II

Intelligence Sources and their Limitations

Air Reconnaissance.

5. This is subject to weather conditions, which may preclude observation over a lengthy and possibly vital period. In Channel coast areas fighter cover has also to be contended with; the fact that air reconnaissance takes place for the most part from 30,000 feet necessarily increases the difficulties of interpretation.

6. Military preparations are more difficult to distinguish by air reconnaissance than naval preparations. Road and rail movements probably take place by night, and even if carried out by day would demand an almost continuous scale of reconnaissance if correct results are to be deduced. The formation of dumps, the construction of roads and road widenings are probably the main indications obtainable.

7. Indications of preparations for seaborne operations are more likely to be obtainable by air reconnaissance than by other means. It must, however, be borne in mind that air reconnaissance is spasmodic and unlikely, therefore, to give a simultaneous estimate of shipping in any large group of ports. Apart from inaccuracies arising from small scale photographs, reconnaissance is also liable to vary in value owing to weather and cloud conditions and the difficulty of covering the large areas of the ports reconnoitred.

The main functions of air reconnaissance are to:—

(*a*) draw attention to changes which have taken place in individual ports indicating the possible imminence of operations;

(*b*) estimate the strength of the threat from a particular port, subject to the reconnaissance being up-to-date and complete.

Secret Intelligence Service.

8. Reports are subject to the usual disadvantages, such as " planting " of inspired information, and delays in transmission. The fact that the occupied territories are to a large extent friendly is offset by the stringent measures which the Germans have taken to exclude unauthorized persons from ports and in some cases from coastal areas.

9. The difficulty of obtaining information is increased by the fact that there is little actual contact with the enemy land forces.

Diplomatic and Political Sources.

10. Diplomatic and political circles are clearly the forcing house of "inspired" information. The greatest care in sifting their reports is necessary, and the information, as far as it concerns enemy intentions, is seldom reliable.

Prisoners' Statements.

11. These are more reliable as regards enemy morale than plans, the latter usually not being known to the junior ranks who form the bulk of the prisoners taken. Their evidence as to preparations actually seen may have some value, but in any event prisoners in present circumstances are almost entirely confined to G.A.F. and naval personnel.

Non-Technical Observers.

12. The technical details of new devices invented by the enemy are important but frequently difficult to obtain owing to observers' lack of the necessary technical knowledge. Reports on "surprise" weapons provide an opportunity for imagination to run riot and are, of course, frequently part of the inspired campaign of horrors and threats.

Distinction of Activities.

13. Difficulties arise in deciding whether certain enemy activities point to invasion or to a continuation of the policy of blockade or even to normal defensive measures; amongst these may be mentioned the installation of heavy guns covering the Straits of Dover, the movement of shipping and barges seen from time to time between the invasion ports, and the changes in the dispositions of the enemy's bomber and fighter forces. A more certain indication would be the disposition of troop-carrying and glider-towing aircraft, but it is unlikely that in the event of operations against the U.K. these would start from coastal areas or even be concentrated in rear areas.

PART III

Enemy Resources and Preparations

(a) *Military*

Distribution of Enemy Forces.

*14. The estimated distribution of enemy forces is shown periodically in War Office Weekly Summaries. In those countries from which military operations in the United Kingdom are likely to be launched the troops present (January, 1942), are for the most part, only sufficient for garrison, coast defence and internal security requirements; major troop movements would, therefore, be necessary before invasion could be attempted. It is probable that concentrations on the coast will be avoided until the last moment, and that railways and M.T. will be used to the maximum for transporting troops to the coast immediately prior to operations.

In view of the fact that shipping is now (January, 1942) distributed throughout the Channel ports, and further large merchant shipping concentrations need not necessarily precede invasion, the reconnaissance of railway movements has assumed greater importance than in September, 1940; there is, in the Low Countries and France, a relatively small number of nodal railway points, periodical reconnaissance of which should give warning of any large scale troop movements.

Dumps.

15. Early in 1941 air reconnaissance of inland areas showed an increasing number of dumps in the PAS DE CALAIS area.

The map at Appendix I shows dumps and other constructional activities in the Low Countries and Northern France as known at beginning of September, 1941. While many of the dumps can be accounted for on various grounds, *e.g.*, G.A.F. and naval requirements, coast defence, or replacement of destroyed oil containers, some of them may be part of the invasion preparations.

Among these are:—

(*a*) Ammunition near the roads and in woods east of ANTWERP.

(*b*) Dumps near the railway suitably sited for supplying AMSTERDAM, ROTTERDAM and ANTWERP.

(c) Dumps on the main line GHENT—OSTEND.

(d) Extensive construction of protected storage in OSTEND (*see* below).

(e) Dumps near the ST. OMER—BOULOGNE and ST. OMER—CALAIS railways, suitably sited for supplying BOULOGNE and CALAIS.

Construction of square concrete shelters has been seen at LE HAVRE, CHERBOURG, BREST, ST. NAZAIRE, OSTEND, DUNKIRK and BOULOGNE. The construction of these shelters, which vary in size but average 50 feet square, began in September, 1940, when German invasion preparations and consequent R.A.F. bombing were at their height. The lack of protection for troops and supplies may have had a deterrent effect on the invasion plan, and the shelters, of which only those at OSTEND are believed to be for personnel, may be intended as a counter-measure.

Long Range Guns.

16. Since September, 1940, the enemy has shown the greatest activity in fortifying strongly with heavy guns the CALAIS—BOULOGNE area. A map showing activities in this area up to 10 September, 1941, will be found at Appendix II.

Reports received state that the range of the guns varies between 65 and 85 miles, and is in some cases as high as 156 miles, but it is not considered that the extreme range exceeds 125 miles. Since these long range guns have come into action, occasional shells have landed 60 miles from the nearest point on the French coast; these firings were obviously not for effect, but for registration or trial purposes.

This distance of 60 miles probably does not indicate the true maximum range of the guns since—

(a) the guns may not be firing with full charge, and

(b) the exact location of the guns firing cannot be positively identified; the guns may be placed some way back from the coast in order that range and accuracy trials can be carried out without disclosing their optimum capabilities.

*17. The calibres so far seem to be between 8½ inches and 12 inches; shells of 28 cm. (11 inches) and 30·5 cm. (12 inches) have been recovered in this country. The life of the guns is not known and cannot with any accuracy be estimated in the absence of information as to the propellant used, but may be in the neighbourhood of 60 rounds. A new type of shell is in use, and this may also have some effect on the life.

It seems probable that approximately 35 long range guns and 100 coast defence guns were available in September, 1941.

It has been reported that there are four 38-cm. (15-inch) Rheinmetall naval guns on turntable mountings near BOULOGNE. No reliable information as to the range of these guns is available, nor have any shell fragments of this calibre been recovered in this country, but air photographs have shown three turntables in the BOULOGNE area suitable for this type of gun.

The accuracy of the long range guns is not equal to that of shorter range field or naval guns, but it is believed that it would be sufficient for the purpose of harassing or destructive fire on areas in the U.K. which cannot satisfactorily be attacked by bomber aircraft. They may, however, be intended mainly for the shelling of convoys and for improving targets for the G.A.F. by limiting the area in the Straits in which shipping can sail. During the last war, the Germans used a 38-cm. (15-inch naval gun) which had a range of at least 46,000 yards (26 miles) and fired a shell of 748 kg. (1,646 lbs.).

A table summarizing particulars of German long range and railway artillery is given in Appendix III.

Gun Emplacements and Positions.

*18. Work was begun on these at the beginning of July, 1940, and carried out at high speed to the exclusion of all other defence work, presumably to be ready in time for the projected German invasion of this country in September, 1940. The work was carried out by the German Labour Corps organization under Dr. Todt, constructor of the Siegfried Line. The first battery of four long range guns on CAP GRIS NEZ took approximately seven weeks to instal, and the first shell, calibre estimated at 30·5 cm. (12 inches), was fired into this country on 18 August, 1940. By mid-September, 1940, 11 long range guns in emplacements and 13 railway gun positions had been located between CALAIS and ETAPLES, and an additional four railway guns on turntable mountings at CHERBOURG.

By mid-September, 1941, there were approximately 35 long range gun positions, including railway turntable mountings and spurs, in the area CALAIS—BOULOGNE.

The long range guns on fixed mountings in the CAP GRIS NEZ area are on high ground, and were installed and serviced by road. They have now been built into extremely strong emplacements with walls approximately 17 feet thick, which provide all-round protection; the distance between these emplacements varies between 120 and 300 yards.

The large number of turntables, approximately 100 feet in diameter, are presumably for long range railway guns of 28 cm. (11 inches) or even 30·5 cm. (12 inches) calibre, which have a very limited traverse of their own.

Four railway guns of smaller calibre, probably 21 cm. (8·27 inches) were seen in September, 1940, on a railway spur running at right angles to the sea. These guns have not been seen in position since.

All fixed long range gun positions are being surrounded by barbed wire entanglements, and a number of pillboxes are sited along the coast. The anti-aircraft defence of the area is very considerable, amounting to some 300 guns between CALAIS and BOULOGNE within five miles of the coast.

Channel Tunnel.

*19. It has been suggested that the enemy might endeavour to effect surprise either by the use of the existing borings for the proposed Channel Tunnel or by the construction of a new tunnel; as regards the former, the position at present is that there are at the foot of the cliffs at GRIS NEZ two vertical borings probably about 8 ft. in diameter. These borings lead to a trial tunnel which probably extends some 1½ to 2 miles out to sea in a curve of approximately 1,000 metres radius; the diameter of the tunnel is about 7 ft. If the similar workings which exist on the English side can be taken as a guide, it is probable that the shafts and the tunnel itself are almost free of water. Up to September, 1939, there were no workings of any kind above the beach level or on the cliffs above, and air reconnaissance has not since disclosed any.

In view, therefore, of the inaccessibility of the entrance to the shafts and the limited nature of the accommodation in the tunnel itself, it is not considered that the enemy is likely to make use of it either for ammunition storage or for any other purpose.

In the opinion of the English Channel Tunnel experts, it is impossible for the Germans even with the most modern equipment to bore a full sized tunnel under the Channel, working from one side only, under a period of some years;

it is in fact, probable that without a foot-hold on this side of the Channel for the necessary triangulation, the task would be an impossible one.

Forces in Norway and Denmark.

*20. Information from NORWAY has been fuller than from FRANCE and the LOW COUNTRIES, but a great deal of the activity reported has been of a defensive nature. On the other hand there has been considerable activity in embarkation and other invasion exercises, including the use of gas, and it must be assumed that NORWAY may be used as a base for a diversion against the north of the U.K. or the FAROES and ICELAND (C).

The activity reported from DENMARK is mostly confined to the ports, and that country must be looked upon as a possible base for naval and air operations. The strength of the forces present in NORWAY and DENMARK is shown in periodical War Office Summaries.

Forces in Germany.

*21. The forces present in GERMANY change constantly and as there is now (January, 1942) no central reserve in that country, it can only be regarded as an area from which drafts can be drawn for any operations in which the German Army is involved.

(*b*) *Naval*

Shipping Resources.

*22. The tonnage of merchant shipping at present (January, 1942) available to Germany is discussed in para. 26.

Germany's barge resources are not likely to exceed some 3,000 self-propelled barges of a type and tonnage suitable for the short seaborne crossing to S.E. ENGLAND in fairly calm weather (*see* para. 33). This crossing would probably be within an area bounded by the lines FLUSHING—THAMES ESTUARY and CHERBOURG—PORTSMOUTH.

Even if shortage of shipping were not a limiting factor in the scale of a German attack launched against this country, there is obviously a limit to the number of craft which can be assembled in any port or convoyed across in one wave. A large part of the total tonnage at Germany's disposal is captured shipping and barges, and it may be presumed that she will have even fewer scruples about risking these craft than she may have about her own.

Location of Shipping.

*23. At Appendix IV, Table 1, will be found a list showing the latest known locations of shipping as shown by air reconnaissance. As emphasized in para. 7, the results are not conclusive, but the list shows the general distribution of shipping at some of the more important ports under German control.

The list is only given as a general guide in what may be considered normal conditions (January, 1942), as opposed to conditions which might precede invasion.

Types Available.

*24. There is not enough evidence to forecast with certainty exactly what types of sea-transport will be used for any particular phase of the operation, but the following are the most important types:—

	Av. speed.
Merchant vessels averaging 4,000 tons ...	12 knots
T.L.Cs. about 650 tons	9-11 ,,
Self-propelled barges averaging 400 tons...	6-8 ,,
Self-propelled barges averaging 120-200 tons	6-8 ,,
Dutch motor coasters between 150-170 tons	9-10 ,,
Siebel ferries	7 ,,

	Av. speed.
Train ferries, 800-3,000 tons...	10-16 knots
Tugs, screw	6 ,,
Barge propulsion craft	6 ,,
Assault craft (fast motor boats, etc.)	20 ,,

The enemy's resources in merchant shipping are dealt with in para. 26, and at Appendix IV, Table 2, is a summary of the numbers of the above craft which may be available now and in April, 1942, respectively.

Use will probably also be made of rafts or lighters for ship to shore transport.

Drawings illustrating several of the "invasion craft" referred to in the following paragraphs will be found at Appendix V.

Categories of Craft.

25. In the following paragraphs is set out a summary of existing information regarding available enemy craft, under four main headings:—

Merchant vessels (M/Vs.).
Barges, T.L.Cs., etc.
Train ferries.
Light craft and rafts.

Merchant Shipping.

*26. Between the Franco-Spanish frontier and the Finnish-Russian Arctic frontier, including the Baltic Sea, it is estimated that Germany has at her disposal approximately 5,350 ships, totalling about 5,000,000 G.R.T. Of these, probably 3,800, totalling approximately 1,000,000 G.R.T., are less than 1,000 G.R.T., leaving 1,550 of approximately 4,000,000 G.R.T. of 1,000 G.R.T. and over. Tankers are included in these figures.

It is assumed that all vessels which are still in occupied territory or which are still controlled by the governments of occupied territory, are at the disposal of Germany whenever she cares to demand their services. In addition, Finnish vessels in this area and French vessels in occupied French ports are regarded as being equally at the disposal of the Germans. In this area, the reserve of shipping which is most readily available to the Germans is the Swedish merchant fleet in the Baltic and North Sea ports. This represents 1,045 ships totalling about 1,000,000 G.R.T., of which 735 ships of about 203,000 G.R.T. are under 1,000 G.R.T.

Even if allowance is made for some incompleteness in the foregoing figures, the number and tonnage of merchant shipping available to Germany still appears to be ample for invasion purposes.

Carrying Capacity of M/Vs.

27. A reasonable basis for calculation of carrying capacity in the case of vessels between 700 and 1,500 tons, is 2 G.R.T. per man. These ships are likely to be used for troops with, possibly, pack animals or motor-cycles, but with little other transport.

For vessels of over 1,500 tons 3 G.R.T. per man is a likely figure, or alternatively 60,000 tons for a division.

For estimating A.F.V. capacity a 4,000-ton merchant vessel could carry 35 light or 16 medium tanks. This load would not be appreciably reduced by the carrying of landing craft as well.

*28. The figures in para. 27 are based on the reduced transport which the enemy might bring in the early stages; an armoured division might bring some 1,100 of its 2,500 vehicles and an infantry division, some 800 of an establishment of 1,800 (M.T. being probably substituted for H.T.). On this basis it is calculated that an armoured division would require some 14 4,000-ton ships and an infantry division some 13 4,000-ton ships.

Formations with their transport drastically reduced in this way would be strictly limited in their radius of action and their use restricted to the bridge-head area.

The re-organization of armoured and infantry divisions referred to in para. 33 is not likely to cause any appreciable modification in the above figures which can, in any case, only be considered approximate.

M/V Tonnage and Identification.

*29. Interpretation reports of photographic reconnaissance usually refer to M/Vs. in terms of their length as measured in the photographs; at Appendix VI and accompanying tables will be found brief notes on M/V categories, relationship between tonnage and length and other information of assistance in identification and classification of M/Vs. which might be used in operations against the U.K. As the speed of M/Vs. has operational significance, a short reference is also made to methods of judging it both visually and in photographs.

Conversion and Adaptation of M/Vs.

30. Relatively few modifications to merchant vessels have been reported. It is believed that some ships have been altered for use in an operation of the "River Clyde" type. This has involved provision of side ports or of openings in the bow closed by a "beak" for the disembarkation of A.F.Vs. and troops into some type of intermediary craft or on to an improvised jetty (*see* sketches at Appendix V). Such an operation, however, imposes limiting factors owing to the inherent difficulties, especially under fire, and the risk of inclement sea conditions. The selection of possible beaches for such an operation is, moreover, somewhat limited. Drawings showing two methods of discharging M.L.Cs. in this manner are at Appendix VII.

Another reported modification is the adaptation of some M/Vs. for the conveyance of up to 30 M.L.Cs. (each already containing its tank or tanks), which can be discharged from the parent ship when the latter is within a short distance of the landing beach.

*31. Normally the main function of merchant vessels would be the disembarkation at a port of troops and equipment following the first phase of the attack. For such a purpose the smaller types of vessel, varying between 1,000 and 4,000 tons according to the class of cargo, would probably be used as giving greater power of manœuvre and at the same time distributing the risk of loss by sinking. Dutch motor coasters (150-170 tons) might also be useful for the conveyance of subsequent supplies. For loading table for 900 and 4,200-ton ships, *see* Appendix VIII.

32. As stated in para. 30, it is possible that merchant vessels have been modified so as to enable troops and stores to be discharged from the bows of the ships; although this might involve certain structural weaknesses in ships not specially designed, it would, if successful, reduce the necessity of capturing port accommodation. Discharge on to a beach, at least in the early stages of an operation, so far from being less convenient than in a port, might offer certain advantages, *e.g.*:—

(*a*) It would postpone the task of capturing one of the few large ports adequate for the enemy's needs.

(*b*) The capture of several small ports would involve heavy calls on the enemy's effort, especially in airborne troops.

(*c*) Roads behind certain long stretches of beach frequently connect more easily with the main road system of a country than the bottleneck roads leading to small harbours, *e.g.*, NEWHAVEN. Railways are in any case unlikely to be available to the enemy at this early stage.

(*d*) The value of captured harbours may be seriously reduced by block ships and other sunken craft, or by destruction of port equipment.

(*e*) Ships run up on to a beach at appropriate intervals of distance are perhaps less vulnerable than vessels crowded alongside the quays of a port.

Invasion Barges.

*33. There are some half-dozen types and sizes of barges in normal use on European waterways, but examination of air photographs shows that a 400-ton dead-weight carrying capacity barge is a reasonable average. This barge is also considered to be the most conveniently sized from the point of view of control and manœuvrability, but in any case it is not considered that a barge of more than 700 tons would be used. Allowing for necessary freeboard for a sea voyage, the load of a 400-ton barge would not exceed 240 tons. Exact calculations have been made allowing for only one row of tanks in each to facilitate rapidity of disembarkation on a beach, as well as for fore and aft strengthening of the hull by truss girders; it is calculated that one armoured division, with a minimum of transport (*vide* para. 28), would require 250 such barges and an infantry division, also with minimum transport, 180 barges, or 238 and 174 respectively if the new organizations used in Russia are used against the U.K. Details of the effects which these changes may have on formations are given in Appendix IX.

*34. There exist large numbers of "Rhine" barges, having a capacity of 1,000 to 3,000 tons, but these are long, cigar-shaped craft, which, even if strengthened, are not suited for sea-going conditions and are, moreover, not self-propelled.

In the event of the supply of the barges described in para. 33 not being sufficient, it is possible that the enemy might make use of some smaller but modern self-propelled barges of between 120 and 200 tons, which are capable of making the Channel crossing; the tank or troop-carrying capacity of these vessels is probably about one-third that of the 400-ton barge.

Self-propelled Barges.

35. The ideal barge for invasion would have some method of self propulsion; a large number of the 400-ton class is so equipped. In the case of those which lack it motor-power might be provided; it is to be noted that, unless specific and somewhat elaborate steps have previously been taken, the motors make a characteristic, periodic and considerable noise, which would probably be audible to the coast defences.

Self-propelled barges offer beaching advantages over towed barges in that their machinery drives them hard up on to the beach and keeps them nosing up; for this reason "dumb" barges would probably be less effective than self-propelled. Also, although Germany probably has some 1,700 screw tugs available, the provision, maintenance and manœuvring of tugs would complicate a large sea-borne operation.

There is little difference in the carrying capacity of towed and self-propelled barges, nor will the capacity be affected in the likely event of the barges being fitted with A.A. guns It is most improbable that any A.A. guns heavier than the 3·7-cm. (1·45-in.) would be used on barges, but very effective defence could be provided by large numbers of 2-cm. (·79-in.) guns; the Germans are known to have ordered several hundreds of these with naval type mountings. The number of barges likely to be towed by tugs in a sea-borne expedition will not exceed two per tug, or one if towed by a self-propelled barge.

Propulsion Craft for Barges.

*36. Information received from Dutch sources indicates that the enemy is developing a new technique for propelling barges. This consists of a small but powerful "propulsion craft", the object of which is to provide power for dumb barges. This is effected by joining two barges together rigidly, and attaching the propulsion craft to the sterns, possibly between them.

Particulars of the craft, so far as known, are:—

Type	Open boat (whether wood or metal unknown).
Length ...	6 m. (20 ft. approx.).
Beam	Same as barge (*i.e.*, 20-25 ft.).
Propulsion ...	Single *water* screw driven by 750 h.p. aero engine centrally placed in the boat.
Speed... ...	Unknown, but unlikely to exceed 6 knots with two barges.
Crew	One man.

These craft have been seen at AMSTERDAM, SCHEVENINGEN, SCHIEDAM and ROTTERDAM. The boats are believed to have been constructed in ROTTERDAM shipyards, where as many as 50 were seen at one time in the early summer of 1941. It is reported that, as batches of the craft are completed, they are sent away and it is possible, therefore, that considerable numbers are available; their small size would facilitate storage and concealment. Exercises, in which this type of craft was used to propel invasion barges, were seen taking place at sea between SCHEVENINGEN and the HOOK OF HOLLAND in September, 1941.

There is no technical objection to this adaptation of a well-known practice, subject to reasonable sea conditions. While it is possible that these craft are intended for use in commercial river traffic, all reports have associated them with invasion barges. It is unlikely that barges so propelled would be used in the early stages of invasion, but a large-scale use of such craft would considerably increase the number of potential invasion barges available to the enemy, as, owing to the disadvantages of using normal tugs, it has not hitherto been considered likely that dumb barges would be used.

Use of Barges.

37. A barge is considered to be seaworthy only for comparatively short sea passages, and its use may, therefore, be expected only across the narrower parts of the North Sea and the Channel (*c.f.* para. 22).

In September, 1940, when invasion appeared imminent, there were in the ports between the Dutch-German frontier and LE HAVRE some 2,500 barges, but as a large proportion of these were in ports which normally have heavy barge traffic, *i.e.*, ROTTERDAM, AMSTERDAM and ANTWERP, it is quite possible that many were required for industrial and normal military purposes.

Description and Capacity of the 400-ton Barge.

*38. A characteristic 400-ton barge as referred to in para. 33 is self-propelled by a Diesel engine, has a speed of 6-8 knots and the following dimensions:—

Length	154 feet.
Beam	16 feet 5 inches.
Depth of hold ...	7 feet 6 inches.
Load draught (commercial load).	6 feet 6 inches.

With a typical military load, the draught would be less, but not greatly so, since it would be necessary to trim the barge by the stern; thus with the barge at its best trim for landing on a fairly flat beach, the draught might be:—

2-3 feet forward.
4 feet amidships.
5-6 feet aft.

Loading table for this type of barge will be found in Appendix VIII.

Tank-Landing Barges.

39. If, as is probably the case, ordinary barges specially adapted for the conveyance of A.F.Vs. form part of the invading force, they will probably consist of two types, of which there is information from photographic and other sources:—the first consists of the fitting of an internal ramp leading up to and over the bows, with a landing flap; the tank mounts the ramp under its own power, and having reached the bow of the barge comes ashore either down a flap hinged to the barge or down a runway slid forward over the bow and dropped on to the beach.

The second and more frequently used method involves the cutting away of a portion of the bow of the barge and the substitution of doors which, on arrival at the beach, open outwards and allow the tank to emerge more or less on the level of the barge bottom. A description and scale drawing based on low-altitude photographs is at Appendix X. Sketches are at Appendix V.

40. The second method, while obviously more convenient from the unloading point of view, has certain disadvantages:

(*a*) The difficulty of ensuring that the doors are watertight.
(*b*) The loss of seaworthiness and manœuvrability owing to the modified shape of the barge.
(*c*) The necessity for the barge to have powerful pumps to correct trim quickly; this involves additional auxiliary power.

Several reports have been received of the armouring of barges with concrete, but it is more likely that the concrete is used on the barge bottom either to make a smooth surface for vehicles over the cross members of the barge or simply as ballast. Reports have also been received of concrete over the top of the barge; this may be an attempt at A.A. protection for personnel, or may indicate the use of barges as pillboxes when beached. These would be probably of about 500 tons with bullet-proof concrete bulwark around a strengthened top deck; the bulwark is believed to contain 10 machine-gun emplacements, and mountings for three light A.A. guns are aligned fore, aft and amidships.

41. A possible method of disembarking tanks from barges might be to remove a section of the bows with oxy-acetylene cutters so that the tank would emerge when the barge grounded on the beach.

It is considered feasible to make certain structural alterations on the barges before sailing, which would reduce the time necessary on arrival for cutting a section out of the bows in order to release the tank. If this were done, it is estimated that it would take four minutes to make an opening from which the tank could emerge; if these preparations were not made it would probably take about 15 minutes.

42. The use of explosives to blow the necessary exit in the bows without risk to tank crews might also be possible. If so, disembarkation could take place almost as soon as the barge grounded.

Special Tank-Landing Craft.

*43. The use of converted barges presents certain inherent difficulties, *e.g.*, the difficulty of ensuring satisfactory co-ordination and timing with barges capable of making only six or seven knots, especially if adverse winds or tides are encountered; the noise factor of the barge engines would also be disadvantageous.

It was, therefore, to be expected that the enemy would, if time allowed, produce in large quantities special A.F.V.-carrying craft, suitable for the first assault, on lines similar to our M.L.Cs. and T.L.Cs. Such a programme was, according to reliable reports (Summer, 1941), prepared for the numerous small ship and barge building yards which abound in the LOW COUNTRIES and FRANCE. Air reconnaissance has confirmed the construction of such craft, but designs still differ, and numbers are small (January, 1942), suggesting that the programme has not yet advanced from the experimental stage to mass production. It is, however, possible that a barge building programme will be put in hand, and it must also be borne in mind that as the craft are constructed they may be moved (whole or in separate portions) inland, where they would not easily be seen.

These steel craft (of which description and sketches will be found in Appendices V and X) are based upon the converted barges previously described, which they resemble in the following particulars:—

(*a*) propulsion aft;
(*b*) unloading from the bow;
(*c*) A.F.V's. loaded in the hold.

This construction programme of special T.L.C.-type craft does not necessarily infer that the many commercial barges already converted will not be used. It is likely, especially in view, of the losses in shipping incurred by the enemy, that these will be utilized for bringing up reinforcements and for conveyance of supplies if and when bridgeheads have been secured. In the meantime considerable use is being made of this type of barge for practice and training purposes, where the relatively slow speed and the noise of the barges is unimportant.

*44. A limited number of barges of a larger type, *viz.*, 210 ft. in length, has been constructed at AMSTERDAM and at other Low Countries shipyards. Definite information as to their construction is not at present available, but they are thought to have bows cut away for tank disembarkation similar to those referred to in paras. 39 and 43; they have, however, certain characteristics which suggest the possibility of their being specially constructed tankers.

Special Barges.

45. Many reliable reports have also been received of " unorthodox " invasion barges. The most important of these are:—

(*a*) Craft with air screws driven by aircraft engines.
(*b*) Barges which can split into three sections each containing an A.F.V. The barge crosses the water as one unit, is then uncoupled and each section (presumably by means of an outboard motor) drives itself up on to the beach.
(*c*) There are indications of independent self-propelled floats being provided for 10-ton Czech tanks.

Air-Screw Propulsion.

*46. Some of the most important experimental work carried out by the enemy on barges has been the use of air-screw propulsion, a technique which is probably better suited to glider types of hull; there is nothing new in the propulsion of light craft by this method, as the Japanese are stated to have used such vessels in landing operations, and they maintain a passenger service on the rivers of Manchukuo with a dish-shaped craft of this kind, 54 ft. by 7 ft. 8 in. by 2 ft. 6 in., with a draught of 3 ft. 10 in.

A picture has also appeared in the German press of a hydro-glider constructed experimentally at COLOGNE. Given a shape of hull in which troops, A.F.V's. or artillery could be accommodated so that the craft would arrive in reasonably good condition, this arrangement might be possible in calm weather. The noise of approach of such a craft would be very great, whilst the vulnerability of the aero-engines is obvious.

This method of propulsion has also been ascribed to some of the twin-hulled craft referred to in para. 47.

The use of air screws to propel a barge, and in particular a pair of barges joined together side by side, must be considered experimental, and the attainment of the high speeds which have been reported in some cases is most unlikely.

It is possible that the Germans, anxious to revive trade on the inland waterways of Europe, may have developed or be experimenting with a special type of fast inland waterway freighter built to do minimum damage to the banks of the canals. There is in any case no evidence that production is on a large scale.

The use of air-screw propelled T.L.C's. or M.L.C's. should also not be ruled out entirely, although such propulsion seems unlikely; sketches of such craft have appeared in the American press showing a box barge-shaped, flat-decked structure, with folding ramp forward and gun turrets.

Twin-Hulled Craft and Siebel Ferries.

*47. Review of the latest evidence relating to these craft points strongly to the " battle ferry " referred to in para. 104, being an improved version of the " Herbert " ferries previously reported. It is also almost certain that both are variations of special twin-hulled craft seen at ANTWERP. The name " Siebel " seems to have replaced the designation " S.S." and is probably the name of the designer. It may also have been adopted in place of " Herbert ", which is strictly applicable only to the pontoons of which these craft are believed to be constructed.

Description, plans and sketches of craft seen and reported are at Appendix XI.

*48. Limited information is available as to the exact use of these craft, but it is known that they are used for carrying 8·8-cm. and 2-cm. Flak artillery, with which they have constantly been associated in reports on trials and exercises. Although air photographs taken at ANTWERP where the craft are assembled and tested have not revealed the presence of guns, the turret-like construction in the centre of the craft is clearly seen (*see* Appendix XI, Fig. 1); the absence of the larger guns might be accounted for by the fact that the majority of the ferries have been seen either during or immediately after assembly. Craft of this type seen at PILLAU, near DANZIG, in July, 1941, had only a 2-cm. (·79-in.) or heavy machine gun mounted on the roofs of the turrets.

Siebel ferries have on occasion been allotted for supplementing Flak defences of a convoy at sea; this task is normally carried out by Flak ships, and, although photographs have shown the ferries exercising with considerable manœuvrability in comparatively smooth waters, it is probable that they would be difficult to handle in a seaway and would therefore be unsuitable for the task. In any case it is considered that, while the 2-cm. guns could not be used against low flying aircraft, the craft would not provide a suitable platform for the use of so heavy a piece as the 8·8-cm. (3·46-in.) gun as a Flak weapon, except in sheltered or calm waters. It is thought that the main uses of this craft are the following:—

(*a*) A platform for an 8·8-cm. (3·46-in.) gun for demolition fire at short range with A.P. ammunition against beach defences and pill-boxes.

(*b*) A platform for 2-cm. (·79-in.) Flak 30 guns to provide defence against low-flying and dive-bombing aircraft and for heavy Flak under suitable conditions.

(*c*) A means for landing heavy Flak 8·8-cm. (3·46-in.) on the beaches, to be used in an established bridgehead in its normal dual-purpose function of Flak and field artillery; for this purpose and for (*a*) the gun may be enclosed in the turret, which would be provided with an opening forward, or it might alternatively be placed in front of the turret; in either case there is a suitable mounting which permits of the gun being fired, at any rate against ground targets, without removal of the four wheels.

(*d*) A means of transporting stores and troops over a short sea crossing and conveying them to beaches, or for lighterage work between ships and the beaches.

(*e*) To be moored in the Channel as a combined Flak platform and large-scale smoke producing apparatus.

There is evidence that considerable importance is attached to the use of this craft as a ferry, and it has been so used in the MEDITERRANEAN and the BALTIC. Siebel ferries at CONSTANZA are reported to have been provided with a ramp forward, and the craft seen at PILLAU had on the decks narrow runways wide enough to take the wheels of a vehicle.

The drawings of the ferries seen at CONSTANZA which are reproduced at Appendix XI, Fig. 2, show that the craft used for ferrying purposes differs materially as regards superstructure from that shown in Fig. 1. The former type carries also in some cases at least one heavy 8·8-cm. (3.46-in.) Flak gun.

A Siebel ferry was in use in October, 1941, as part of the defences of SOLA aerodrome, Norway (*see* Appendix XI, para. 3 and Figs. 3 and 4). As will be seen from the reproduction of a photograph, the superstructure resembles that of the ANTWERP type, but the armament consists of three 8·8-cm. (3·46-in.) and two 2-cm. (·79-in.) Flak guns; it is possible that, in order to distinguish them from the types used for ferrying, the heavily armed types are termed "Kampf Faehren" (battle ferries).

The fact that the enemy has thought it necessary to provide heavy Flak in craft suitable for beaching suggests that his tactics will be to use principally T.L.Cs., barges and other small craft for beach landings; any specially prepared M/Vs. and similar large vessels which are intended to run aground would themselves be strong enough to carry the heavy Flak which small craft are unable to do.

The continuous constructional activity at ANTWERP over a long period, coupled with their suitability for transport and concealment and their presence both in the BALTIC and the MEDITERRANEAN, makes it possible that a considerable number of these craft has been constructed.

Train and Car Ferries.

49. Ferries, although not numerous, are worthy of attention because they are seaworthy in almost any conditions and are most suitable for the conveyance of A.F.Vs. and M.T.; they are also of relatively high speed. There are in enemy hands at the moment some 25 such ferries, this figure comprising 5 German owned, 15 Danish, 2 Norwegian and 3 of unknown nationality, possibly Dutch. The Swedish ferries operating on the SASSNITZ-TRELLEBORG route have not been included. Reports have been received of the

Dutch railway ferries being fitted with 75-ft. ramps for disembarkation of A.F.Vs. The capacity of the 2,700-ton type might be 1,500 men and 30-40 medium tanks.

Particulars of typical German and Scandinavian ferries are given in Appendix XIII. For sketch, *see* Appendix V.

In addition to those shown, there are a great number of car ferries in use on the big German rivers, none of which, however, could be used except in a flat calm sea.

Light Craft and Rafts.

50. The various types which may be used can be referred to under various headings, *viz.*:—

Assault craft.
Special rafts.
Trawlers and coasters.
Fishing craft.

Assault Craft.

51. Under this heading may be regarded those ships or boats which rely on their speed, armour and armament to land the first waves of troops on a beach, and on their shallow draft to cross minefields and shoals. They fall naturally under two sub-headings:—

(*a*) Those sufficiently seaworthy to carry assaulting troops from the embarkation ports to the English coast. No reliable estimate of the total numbers of such craft can be made, as there is insufficient evidence, but it would be feasible for the Germans to build in considerable numbers motor boats capable of doing 25 knots in a moderate sea, each carrying some 20 or more men. Many and varying reports on these lines have been received, including references to 80-ton vessels (similar to the German E boat, *i.e.*, motor torpedo boat) capable of 15 knots and carrying 240 men.

(*b*) Boats which must be carried in transports, and are likely when launched to be extremely fast and difficult to hit; the fact of their being so carried tends to diminish the degree of surprise which the enemy will be able to achieve.

52. Use may be possibly made in smooth water of special craft similar to the Japanese craft described in para. 46; their speed (in smooth river water) is about 40-50 knots.

53. Apart from these specially constructed boats, it is possible that the " Sturmboote " (assault boats) forming part of the normal equipment of engineer battalions may be used. A description of these will be found in Appendix XIV. Large numbers can be transported in a small space, and their high speed makes them ideal for landing engineer and other assault troops from ships; they could probably not be handled in any seaway.

Special Rafts.

54. These are easily and cheaply built, and the enemy is known to have prepared and practised with many types; the main use to which these might be put is probably to form jetties or landing stages at the beaches. Reports of rafts being fitted with outboard motors suggest that they might also be used for the conveyance of troops and equipment between larger vessels and the shore, although they would obviously be vulnerable targets.

Types and Uses of Rafts.

55. There have been numerous reports of rafts, many of them unsubstantiated, and it is impossible to discuss all the types which have been tried, but the following are of interest:—

(*a*) " Landungsfloesse " are timber and barrel rafts 13 feet to 15 feet long. The centre is hollowed out to take a quick-firing gun. It is suggested that this may be 8·1-cm. (3·16-in.) mortar, 3·7-cm. (1·45-in.) A.Tk. gun or 7·5-cm. (2·95-in.) infantry gun.

(*b*) Wooden pontoons have been reported carrying metal-covered wooden platforms to be embarked or towed for the off-loading of mechanized vehicles. These pontoons fit into each other bow to stern and may be a possible means of ship-to-shore transport.

(*c*) Reports have also been received of small " T " shaped craft or rafts fitted with aero-engines; one such craft reported is described as having two boat-shaped hulls with a " T " shaped platform superimposed, a structure vaguely described as a " bridge " amidships, and three aero-engines on the head of the " T "; there is no indication as to which is the bow. Steering would be accomplished by varying the speeds of the outer engines. In view, however, of the small dimensions of this craft (*viz.*: 25 feet by 20 feet approximately), it is felt that its use must be restricted to operations close inshore.

T-Shaped Rafts.

*56. A number of large " T " shaped rafts (*see* Appendix XII) were first seen under construction at STICKENHORN, KIEL, in July, 1940, and subsequently at other German North Sea and Baltic ports and at several of the principal ports in Norway. In all cases they have been associated with ports which are either predominantly naval or handle a quantity of naval shipping.

These units appear to be timber frameworks, encasing six buoyancy tanks each about 24 ft. long and probably of metal, on which some timber superstructure may be built, often in the form of a lattice-work screen.

Due probably to the use of local materials, the design of rafts seen at STRAVANGER and KRISTIANSAND differ in minor details from those constructed at German ports.

In Norway they have been constructed in small numbers at STAVANGER and three of them were seen in August being carried athwartships in a merchant vessel from STAVANGER to BERGEN. The increasing use of BERGEN as a naval port makes the arrival of " T " shaped rafts in this port consistent with their previous record of appearances.

There is little doubt that they are rafts in the true sense of the word; they have frequently been seen joined together end to end in which form they could be used as a ship to shore landing stage. The smoothest weather conditions would, however, be necessary to make this practicable.

At KIEL, WILHELMSHAVEN and SWINEMUNDE, they have been seen in use as a boom; air photographs of SWINEMUNDE, taken in mid-September, 1941, showed a boom constructed of " T " shaped rafts, stretching half-way across the entrance channel.

They have also been used (at WILHELSHAVEN only) as camouflage rafts, the superstructure being specially modified.

The number of these rafts so far constructed cannot be estimated accurately, but is probably a minimum of 400.

It is interesting to note the complete absence of these rafts from the invasion ports in the Low Countries and France and from the French Atlantic ports.

Trawlers and Coasters.

57. The total number of these vessels (all under 1,000 tons) available to the enemy is not known, but they certainly include 400 which were previously Dutch owned and whose crews, if their services were impressed, could make use of an intimate knowledge of the English coast. These craft have a speed of about 9 knots, a draught of 8 feet and could carry some 100 men and personal equipment.

Although no definite figures are available, it is estimated that there are sufficient vessels to transport some four or five divisions without equipment; their distribution is very general. For sketches *see* Appendix V.

Fishing Craft.

58. There has been a number of reports of Norwegian and Breton fishing boats of between 30 and 50 tons being adapted for transport of military stores and even A.F.Vs. It is, however, considered that the use of these craft is improbable except during spells of the calmest weather.

59. Finally, there are great numbers of wooden fishing vessels about 60 feet long, drawing 8-9 feet, and having auxiliary motors giving a speed of about 7-9 knots. Some of these are reported to have been modified to carry one light tank, but very steep beaches would be necessary for landing. Such a vessel could take about 20 equipped men in addition to the crew, but in this case at least, if not in some of the others mentioned, the possibility of sea-sickness is a real factor, and except during the most favourable weather conditions their use would be restricted to short sea passages. For sketches *see* Appendix V.

German Naval Units.

60. The use which the enemy may make of his fleet is largely an operational matter, and intelligence can give few indications of likely action except in so far as present constructional activities are concerned. It is safe to say that the enemy has constructed many of the smaller type of units for conveying and covering a seaborne expedition, *e.g.*, destroyers, submarines, E boats (small motor torpedo boats) and R boats (small mine sweepers). For description of the two last-named, *see* Appendix XV.

The function of the bigger German units may possibly be to draw off the British Fleet by making a diversion (*e.g.*, by attacking Ireland or by raiding in the Atlantic) and then returning in time to aid the main attack. Regular reconnaissance of German naval ports is likely to furnish the only indications of such operations.

61. The probable tasks of the German Navy can be summarised as:—

(*a*) *Close support of the main invasion.*

Destroyers, E boats, A.A. ships and M/S craft.

(*b*) *Flank support of the communications.*

Minefields, S/M patrols and light forces up to and possibly including cruisers.

(*c*) *Cover to a diversionary expedition.*

Heavy ships, carriers and possibly cruisers.

In addition it is possible that the two old battleships (SCHLESWIG-HOLSTEIN and SCHLESIEN) will be employed in close support of the main invasion and at a later stage as temporary coastal batteries at the English bridgehead. These ships may have their main armament removed and be fitted with improved HA/LA armament.

*62. The estimated strength of the German Fleet at 31/12/41 is shown in Appendix XVI.

The number and armament of German E boats is likely to be an important factor in a seaborne attack. The number likely to be available in March, 1942, at the present rate of construction is estimated to be about 110, but their present armament is unsuitable. It is probable, therefore, that the production of E boats will be intensified and that existing ones will be re-armed with a more effective gun (probably using incendiary ammunition).

(*c*) *Air.*

Disposition of G.A.F.

63. The outstanding feature of enemy activity has been the lavish construction of new aerodromes and the extension of old aerodromes, especially the provision of runways for taking off with heavy loads.

This is known to have taken place generally in occupied territories, but as a result of the priority in air reconnaissance assigned to the areas behind the Channel and North Sea ports, much information is available as to the activity which the enemy has shown there; on the other hand this work cannot be associated exclusively with invasion as opposed to blockade.

Establishment and Operational Strength.

*64. The latest estimated figures of the strength of the G.A.F. are given at Appendix XVII.

The main G.A.F. types of operational and transport aircraft are shown at Appendix XVIII, and map of their radii of action at Appendix XIX.

Maximum Strength.

65. It is possible that, in the last resort, as a final gamble Germany might make use of the whole of her air forces, which might amount to about 13,000 aircraft, including 1,200 transport aircraft. Sufficient aerodromes for operating this number of aircraft are available, but although the morale might be very high at first such an unnaturally inflated force would be relatively inefficient. It can be assumed that indications would be received beforehand of preparations for such an operation.

Organization of Airborne Troops.

*66. The organization and equipment of German airborne troops, as far as is known at present is as follows:—

(*a*) German parachute troops are G.A.F. personnel. There are believed to be also some Army parachute troops (*e.g.*, one company in a mountain rifle regiment), but no large formations of these are known.

(*b*) German airlanding troops are Army troops (infantry or mountain infantry) selected for some special operation and specially trained in emplaning and deplaning. The only exception is the Gliderborne Regiment composed of G.A.F. personnel who receive special training as shock troops; though technically airlanding troops, gliderborne troops work with and are equipped like parachute troops.

Parachute and Gliderborne Troops.

*67. All airborne operations are controlled by XI Air Corps (Fliegerkorps) which, apart from normal complement of signals, transport, etc., falls into two sections:—

(*a*) air transport.
(*b*) airborne troops.

The air transport side of XI Air Corps is composed of three Transport Groups (Geschwader) of Ju. 52 aircraft and several additional wings, together with one Airlanding Group of similar composition. The Airlanding Group trains with, and has operated with gliders.

Each Group contains 3 or 4 Wings (Gruppe) (total up to 220 aircraft).

Each Wing contains 4 Squadrons (Staffel) (total 53 aircraft).

Each Squadron contains 12 aircraft.

The total number of aircraft is not less than 750. About 650 were actually employed in CRETE, and finally transported about 30,000 men by ferrying over a considerable period against weak opposition.

The total number of Ju. 52s available to Germany may be about 1,500, but the majority of these are not organized in any formation; those in XI Air Corps are normally dispersed and employed on ordinary transport duties. (*See* also Appendix XVII, para. 3.)

*68. Airborne troops of XI Air Corps are composed of:—

Parachute troops.

Corps troops	2,000
7 Air Division (Fliegerdivision 7)—	
Divisional troops	2,000
Three parachute rifle regts. of 2,000 each	6,000

Gliderborne troops.

One assault regt. 2,000

Total—
10,000 parachute troops.
2,000 gliderborne troops.

At Appendix XX are details of:—

(*a*) Composition of above formations.
(*b*) Equipment carried.
(*c*) Aircraft required for transport.

*69. Parachute troops are liable to very heavy casualties. Reserves are correspondingly large and training of infantry in parachute jumping may have reached saturation point. There does not appear to be any important difference between the parachute regiments referred to in the preceding paragraph and the very large numbers of other infantry (probably not less than 100,000) who are believed to have undergone parachute courses.

It is believed that even if Germany's fleet of transport aircraft were expanded, the enemy would not at present undertake an airborne operation needing more *parachute* troops than those at present in XI Air Corps, though more gliderborne troops might be created, and considerable use would, of course, be made of airlanding troops.

Airlanding Troops.

*70. Units of most arms and services can be armed and equipped for air transport, and can speedily be trained to emplane and deplane.

At Appendix XXI the organization of the airlanding division as used in HOLLAND is given, but there is no reason to suppose that this is standardized, *e.g.*, in CRETE mountain troops were used as being suitable to the nature of the country involved; the organization has in any case probably been improved upon. The heavier weapons which can now be carried are referred to in para. 80.

Attention is drawn to the main differences between this airborne division and the normal German infantry divisions; these are as follows:—

(*a*) The strength is approximately only 50 per cent. of the normal infantry division; the effective fighting strength, however, is not greatly affected.
(*b*) Two instead of the normal three infantry regiments.

(*c*) A higher percentage of riflemen and a smaller percentage of supporting weapons.
(*d*) No artillery of a greater calibre than the 7·5-cm. (2·95-in.) mountain gun.
(*e*) Skeleton supply services.
(*f*) A higher proportion of officers and non-commissioned officers.
(*g*) No transport vehicles.

All airlanding troops are likely to be used only in large scale operations in co-operation with parachute and glider-borne troops.

Gliders.

*71. Gliders can land where aircraft cannot, and have the added advantage of silent approach, but are difficult to handle when towed in cloud or in conditions of poor visibility. It is probable, therefore, that towing or landing at night would be a difficult operation unless visibility were fairly good. (*See* also para. 124.)

Information of a technical nature based upon the latest information will be found in Appendix XXII as follows:—

(*a*) Technical details (including extracts from German glider range-tables).
(*b*) Drawings of troop-carrying gliders D.F.S. 230 and Gotha 242.

Conveyance of light tanks by means of glider is possible, and the latest available information on this subject is given in paragraph 79 and in Appendix XXII, para. 10.

Disposition of Aerodromes.

*72. The number of aerodromes and landing grounds in N.W. Europe now available to the enemy for use in an airborne invasion of England is now so great that they no longer constitute a limiting factor. Ample accommodation for troop-carrying and glider-towing aircraft is available within range of our East and South-East coasts, without having recourse to the main operational bases which will be required for the bomber, dive bomber and fighter units taking part in the operation.

Airborne invasion does not necessarily entail the need for large aerodromes equipped with runways; unless future development of G.A.F. gliders involves fresh technical considerations, this view is supported by the following facts:—

(*a*) the majority of enemy aerodromes on which gliders have so far been photographed have not been equipped with runways, and are frequently quite small in size.

(*b*) the largest scale airborne operation so far effected by the enemy, the invasion of CRETE, was carried out from Greek aerodromes which had no runways.

The enemy has every inducement *not* to employ his larger operational bases for loading airborne troops in order (*a*) to avoid overcrowding his other operational units; (*b*) to reduce, as far as possible, the risk of inquisitive aerial reconnaissance.

It is considered most improbable that the aerodromes from which an airborne invasion might be launched would be situated in any " forward " area (such as the Pas de Calais or along the Belgian-Dutch coast), for the following reasons:—

(*a*) Such aerodromes would almost certainly be reserved exclusively for the use of short-range aircraft taking part in the operations.

(*b*) A comparison of the distance from base to objective in the invasion of Crete with the corresponding distance from the Continent to the middle of Kent and to Norwich, shows that a large area of N.W. France and almost the whole of Holland falls within this range.

(*c*) Ample accommodation is available on good landing-grounds (not normally in operational use), situated in the backward part of this area, to which airborne troops, gliders and transport aircraft could be moved immediately prior to the invasion, with the minimum risk of detection and interference.

PART IV

EXERCISES AND SPECIAL WEAPONS

(a) *Combined Operations*

Embarkation Exercises.

73. Reports show that since June, 1940, the enemy has consistently carried out embarkation and disembarkation exercises along the whole of the coastline from NORWAY to the ATLANTIC coast. These exercises have been with and without tanks, and have in particular made use of specially prepared craft, *e.g.*, rafts, modified trawlers, etc. ANTWERP appears to have been one of the main scenes of these activities.

While undue weight must not be given to the numerous reports of losses incurred during these exercises, it can at least be said that they are not popular with German troops, a fact which may have some bearing upon the morale of an invading force.

Cliff-Climbing Exercises.

74. Reported exercises in cliff-climbing suggest that such an operation may be undertaken, assisted by parachute parties landed on the top of cliffs with special hauling tackle and apparatus. This operation must necessarily be slower than the normal, and at present excludes the use of tanks; it will probably only be undertaken, therefore, as a subsidiary part of a larger landing, to place ashore forces whose rôle would be to work round to the main beaches and attack the defences in the rear.

Asbestos Clothing and Extinguishers.

*75. A number of reports have been received stating that, amongst other invasion exercises, German troops have been made to practise swimming through water covered with burning oil; for this purpose, troops taking part in the exercise have been equipped with special light weight asbestos suits.

Perhaps the most important conclusion to be drawn from these reports is that the Germans at least have the idea that burning oil may form a part of the beach defences of this country.

It is possible that the reports may have become garbled and that the asbestos was in fact used to line completely enclosed invasion barges so as to give protection from flames to troops inside; each barge might be provided with its own oxygen supply for breathing while crossing the belt of flames.

Boats fitted with foam type extinguishers are also reported to have been used; little credence is attached to these reports as it is considered that the attack on burning oil from boats approaching the leeward side would be very difficult even if personnel were wearing asbestos suits. The maximum range of a foam branch pipe is under 50 ft. and the temperature at that distance from the edge of the fire would be over 100° C. in a moderate wind and higher in a heavy wind. Moreover, the size and weight of any foam extinguisher that would be efficacious in extinguishing burning oil on the sea are such that the boats to be used would have to be of very considerable dimensions. The apparatus could not in any case be used except in a flat calm.

Technically there is no doubt that asbestos suits would afford some protection to troops having to cross a barrier of this type, but it would probably be necessary to provide every man with an individual self-contained oxygen supply in order to allow him to breathe either whilst submerged in the water or whilst actually traversing the burning oil. This would be quite possible. Moreover, although it would undoubtedly constitute a severe test for any troops to swim any distance encumbered in this way, it is pointed out that the men may be specially selected and the asbestos suit might well be the only clothing worn.

Amphibious Tanks.

76. There is ample evidence that the German Army has been paying exceptional attention to the development of this type of A.F.V. Reports have varied, the types reported ranging from the light 5-ton to super-heavy vehicles of over 100 tons.

The only type of which details are known is the 6½-ton Czech model, but the number of these available to the enemy is not known; these tanks have a crew of three and an armament of one heavy machine gun.

Numerous reports suggest that the Germans have been developing heavier amphibious tanks, and while 10-16 tons is likely to be the most common size, types up to 40 tons may quite well be in production.

The movement of amphibious tanks across the Channel or the North Sea under their own power is very problematical, and it is, therefore, reasonable to assume that any amphibious tank now developed for production in large numbers would be of such a size that it would be carried across the sea in a ship or tank-landing craft and only use its amphibious qualities for the last stage of the journey. This would bring the practical size down to about 30 tons, and the commonest type would probably be about 12-16 tons.

It should also be borne in mind that the flotation gear necessary would make very large amphibians awkward vehicles to manœuvre on dry land (unless the flotation gear could be discarded on landing), and that they would present definite disadvantages when compared with normal heavy tanks, which could quite well be landed from sea-borne craft.

Submarine Tanks.

77. Tanks which can travel along the sea-bed and surprise the defenders by emerging on the beaches have been the subject of a number of reports.

One report states that the Germans have built 1,600 of these submarine tanks to be driven by accumulators and carried near to the English coast on rafts and barges, whence they will proceed under their own power.

Another report says that a vacuum is created in the vehicle and the crew are equipped with special breathing apparatus. These tanks cross the water not by floating, but on the bottom; this is feasible, but, due to the difficulty of underwater propulsion, their use would probably be restricted to fairly narrow stretches of water.

The requisite batteries for high underwater endurance would be both cumbersome and heavy, and the problem of water tightness and navigation would have to be solved as in the submarine. The practical difficulties of construction would be considerable, if the vehicle were required to withstand pressures at more than moderate depths.

In spite of the constructional difficulties, the idea behind these reports should not be discarded as impracticable. It is not beyond the Germans to have devised and brought such a machine to a practical possibility, within the limits suggested.

Airborne Tanks.

78. There is no doubt that the Germans have devoted a great deal of attention to the transport of tanks by aircraft.

The limiting factor is the weight and bulk which an aircraft can carry, and it is believed that while the maximum weight possible at present is 10 tons, this would be slightly reduced in practice by dimensional restrictions.

It would thus be possible to transport the Pz. Kw. I (5·7 tons) or the Pz. Kw. II (9 tons), the tank entering and leaving the fuselage by a ramp. Alternatively, three Czech S. I 3½-ton tanks could be carried.

The only known German aircraft suitable for carrying such heavy loads is the Ju. 90, of which it is believed Germany possesses only 30.

Germany has, however, a large number of Ju. 52's, which can carry up to 3½ tons. They could be adapted to carry the 2½-ton Polish T.K. tank, or specially designed very light tanks of which there have been a number of reports. The fighting performance of these light tanks would not be very high, and they would be vulnerable to "tank hunters" and A.Tk. rifles.

Reports have been received of tanks carried slung from aircraft, of very light tanks of about one ton weight being carried by gliders, and even being dropped by parachute. Experiments have no doubt been carried out on these lines, but it is thought that at present these methods are unlikely to prove practicable.

Brief particulars of possible German airborne tanks are given in Appendix XXIII.

During the CRETE operation the "tracked motor cycle" was taken by air in small numbers: this is really a small semi-tracked tractor of 30 h.p. but it might be mistaken for a small A.F.V. or chenillette.

Glider-Borne Tanks.

*79. It has been reported that a glider-borne tank has been produced; it is stated to be a specially designed tank to which are attached temporary wings, tail and aero engine which can be automatically discarded on landing.

The gliding angle, due to the drag of the unfaired tank, would probably be slightly steeper than for the more conventional type of glider carrying a tank in its fuselage. This might account for the use of the suggested auxiliary engine to flatten the descent path, but such a procedure seems to be unwarranted, unless the tank is designed expressly for the purpose.

Other reports have referred to light two-man tanks, but the method of flight described has varied. Some maintain that they are carried by a specially constructed glider, in which the tank more or less forms both the fuselage and the under-carriage. As soon as the glider comes down the wings fall away leaving the tank to continue under its own power; the glider would be towed by a Ju. 52.

It has also been stated that many thousands of these gliders and tanks have been manufactured, and that experiments have been carried out for carrying much larger tanks.

Tanks of about 3 tons landed by glider are unlikely to be heavily armed or armoured, but owing to the large number of possible landing places they might have a considerable nuisance value.

Air photographs show the existence of very large gliders with a span of about 180 feet; these gliders are probably experimental, but it is possible that they have been designed with a view to carrying heavy supply loads and/or tanks (*see* also Appendix XXII, para. 10).

Airborne Guns.

*80. Full details of guns which can be carried in aircraft or gliders will be found in Appendix XXXII. Particular attention is drawn to Serial 4, the 2-cm. (·79-in.) Model 41 Anti-Tank gun which is very efficient, and to Serial 17, the 15-cm. (5·91-in.) Heavy Infantry Howitzer which is a heavy weapon. The 5-cm. (1·97-in.) A.Tk. gun (Serial 8) is one of the best in the German Army. The production of the "tracked motor cycle" for haulage, which is easily taken by air, has made possible the use of these heavier weapons.

Rockets.

81. Reports have been received from time to time indicating that the Germans have, for some years, been paying attention to the development of rockets. Certain of these reports suggest that more recent study has been in the direction of using them as a support weapon for invasion.

The suggestion that the rockets could be used as a long-range gun firing from the other side of the Channel can probably be discounted. On the other hand, there are certain advantages in the use of rocket projectiles from small craft such as the Germans are generally considered likely to use in an invasion. These advantages can be summarized as follows:—

(*a*) They can be fired from small craft which would not be strong enough to withstand the discharge of a gun of comparable calibre.

(*b*) Their high rate of fire would, to some extent, compensate for the lack of accuracy obtainable from floating mountings unprovided with special stabilizing devices.

(*c*) They could be used for developing an intense bombardment of the coast with H.E. smoke or gas during the approach of landing craft.

(*d*) The projectors would be much more easily transported to the shore than equivalent artillery pieces, and they would, therefore, provide good supporting fire in the early stages of land operations.

This use of rockets in combined operations is a conjecture supported by reports and the above considerations. It might well offer a solution to the problem of providing adequate artillery support, which, owing to the lack of suitable naval craft, would not otherwise be available.

Flame-Throwers.

82. Reports have been received indicating that flame-throwers have been used during certain phases of specialized invasion training carried out by the enemy.

The flame-throwers are reported to be mounted on boats and to have a range of from 50 to 300 metres; for various reasons, however, it is considered more probable that if flame-throwers are used in this connection at all, they are more likely to be of the one-man portable type rather than fixed flame-throwers mounted on boats.

It is considered that the upper practical limit of a flame-thrower's range is in the neighbourhood of 150 yards; a flame-thrower mounted on a boat standing off-shore is not likely to find a target on shore within this range. Moreover, the flame-thrower, with its pumping motor and fuel storage tank, would represent a volume and weight (the discharge rate of a jet giving 150 yards range is of the order of 2½ tons of fuel per minute) which attacking craft could probably ill afford for a weapon of such doubtful value.

Once troops and A.F.Vs. taking part in a landing have disembarked and are on the beaches, an assault on the anti-tank obstacles and defence positions becomes a normal land operation, in which German troops are well trained. Flame-throwers, particularly the portable type, have been used extensively in operations during the present war, and assault troops undoubtedly have extensive training in the use of this weapon; it is quite reasonable, therefore, that flame-throwers would be seen in use during landing practice. The portable type has the advantage of flexibility, though its maximum range under favourable conditions is only 20 yards. Reliable details of the tank-mounted flame-thrower are lacking, but it can be taken to have a range of anything up to 150 yards with a duration of jet of one to two minutes.

There is no doubt that without a covering smoke screen the use of flame-throwers against resolutely defended and properly sited defensive positions is a hazardous operation. The range of either the portable or the tank mounted type is relatively short, and it should be possible to prevent flame-throwers approaching sufficiently near to their target to enable them to open fire.

Remote-Controlled Land Torpedoes.

83. A weapon which it is known the Germans were developing during the early stages of the war is a remote controlled land torpedo for the destruction of fortifications and defence works. German developments were on the lines of a small tracked vehicle, streamlined and approximately 3 feet in height, propelled by a petrol engine and carrying a heavy charge of explosive. Detonation took place a few seconds after the forward movement of the vehicle had been arrested by an obstacle, or when the operator gave a tug on a trailing cable; this arrangement was the only remote control feature of the torpedo.

The French were also developing similar land torpedoes and in particular had designed an extremely efficient battery-driven vehicle known as Vehicle K. This was very small and carried only 90 lbs. of explosive, but could be controlled as to speed and direction and moment of detonation by a 3-core trailing cable. This vehicle was also capable of moving under water, provided the bottom was reasonably level and firm. Tests had also been carried out by the French with wireless-controlled tankettes, but although the wireless control feature was quite successful, they were for other reasons not so successful as Vehicle K.

The French designs undoubtedly fell into German hands at the time of the occupation, and it is reasonable to suppose that, with the particular purpose of invasion in view, they would be likely to have incorporated the best features of the French designs into their own. It is possible, therefore, that they now have a tankette which can be launched from off-shore and under wireless control be capable of advancing up the beach and being detonated when the first obstacle is reached. An attack with a number of these weapons released simultaneously from landing craft while still a little way off shore would constitute a formidable preparation for the main tank attack.

On the other hand there are definite limitations to the use of vehicles of this type, the chief of which is that owing to their small size it is impossible for the operator to judge their position exactly, and he can be said to have no effective control at a range of over 500 yards. These small tankettes can also be arrested in front of the main line of obstacles either by a comparatively small ditch or by one or two rows of dannert wire. They also require reasonably level going, both under water and on dry land, and can easily be stopped by rocks and inequalities in the ground.

Full size tanks filled with explosive and arranged for remote control might also be used; these might get through wire but would detonate anti-tank mines. Against either small or large remote control vehicles the use of smoke is of assistance to the defence, since the operator can no longer control his vehicle, and if a gap is blown in the defence line it is difficult to locate it exactly.

Assault Guns.

*84. Two types of assault gun have so far been identified, the 7·5-cm. (2·95-in.) tank gun mounted on a Pz. Kw. III chassis, and the 15-cm. (5·91-in.) infantry gun on a Pz. Kw. I chassis.

The 7·5-cm. (2·95-in.) assault gun has a very squat appearance, while the 15-cm. (5·91-in.) assault gun has a high built-up, box-like shield on front and sides.

Assault artillery is organized in independent batteries in the G.H.Q. pool, and is allotted to corps and divisions, when required for special close support tasks. An assault gun battery might well be attached to an armoured or motorized division for an initial landing.

Assault guns are well suited to operate with motorized or lorried infantry. They may be employed when some special centre of resistance is to be overcome and also for fighting in built-up areas.

Anti-Tank Guns on S.P. Mountings.

*85. German anti-tank guns on S.P. mountings are:—

2-*cm.* (0·79-*in.*) *Super Heavy M.G.*—Penetration 40-mm. (1·57-in.) homo-hard plate at 200 yds. at 20 degrees. This is mounted on a semi-tracked carrier.

4·7-*cm.* (1·85-*in.*) *S.P. A.Tk. Gun.*—Penetration 60-mm. (2·36-in.) armour at 220 yds. at normal. This is mounted in the Pz. Kw. I (5·7-ton) tank with normal turret removed and a special superstructure substituted.

8·8-*cm.* (3·46-*in.*) *A.A./A.Tk. Gun.*—Penetration 100-mm. (3·94-in.) armour at 400 yds. at 30 degrees.

Battalions of A.Tk. guns on S.P. mountings are G.H.Q. units allotted to corps and divisions where required.

It appears that in addition to the German 5·7-ton Pz. Kw. I tanks, numbers of which have been rendered surplus by the re-organization of Germany's armoured divisions and have been utilized for mobile anti-tank weapons, the Germans are converting in French factories certain types of French tanks into these self-propelled gun mountings; conversion seems to follow the lines of similar modifications to the German tanks, *i.e.*, the turret is removed and a gun and shield fitted in its place.

The following types of tanks suitable for this purpose were in existence and in production at the time of the Armistice:—

Renault, A.M.R.	4½ tons weight	speed 31 m.p.h.
Renault, R. 35	11 tons weight	speed 12½ m.p.h.
Hotchkiss H. 35	11½ tons weight	speed 17 m.p.h.

The French also possess a gun tank, the Somua, S. au 40, mounting one 7·5-cm. (2·95-in.) gun, 40-mm. (1·57-in.) armour, 21½ tons weight, with maximum speed of 18 m.p.h.

New Anti-Tank Gun Model 41.

*86. This weapon which was originally referred to by the Germans as " Schwere Panzer Büchse 41 " (heavy anti-tank gun 41) doubtless for security reasons, is the first gun designed on the Gerlich principle to be put into service. The gun is light and highly mobile, and can be easily transported by air complete or by parachute, as it can, if necessary, be dismantled into the following parts:—

Cradle and trigger housing.
Frame and mounting.
Axle and wheels.
Front shield.
Rear shield (clips on to front shield for transport).
Barrel and recoil brake.

The muzzle velocity is reported to be extremely high (6,250 ft./sec.). A mean M.V. of about 4,555 ft./sec. was recorded during trials in this country, but the gun tested was worn, and the original M.V. was no doubt higher. No allowance for travel of target is necessary at ranges up to 500 yds. owing to the short time of flight of the projectile. The gun is serviced by a crew of five who have to wear ear protectors. The barrel is constructed on the Gerlich principle and tapers from 28 mm. at the breech to 20 mm. at the muzzle. Length of barrel is 61·5 in. Penetrations are as follows:—

76·2-mm. (3-in.) machineable plate at 100 yds. at normal.

60-mm. (2·36-in.) face-hardened plate at 200 yds. at 30 degrees.

50-mm. (1·97-in.) homo-hard plate at 300 yds. at normal.

Amphibious Troop Carrier.

*87. Reports, so far unconfirmed, have been received that the Germans are experimenting with an amphibious troop carrier; the particulars given are inconclusive, but indicate that the vehicle is somewhat similar to the U.S.A. "Roebling Alligator" amphibious troop carrier.

Details reported were as follows:—

Length	24 ft.
Width	10 ft.
Height	12 ft.
Speed (roads) ...	20 m.p.h.
Engine	Not visible, but believed to be petrol rather than Diesel.
Track	Flat plates, 10 in. wide, appeared thin and light in weight.

Estimated capacity 36 fully equipped troops.

Two propeller shafts extended through the rear of the body hull. Each shaft was about 30 inches from the side-wall of the vehicle. Each propeller consisted of two blades, each about 20 inches long. A rudder, about 24 inches high and 18 inches wide, appeared to be attached to the rear of each propeller shaft housing.

The sides of the upper part of the hull extended out over the tracks. The lower forward section of the hull curved upward at an angle of approximately 45°. The entire forward section of the hull presented a blunt appearance.

The upper edge of the hull was encircled by a 1½-in. or 2-in. rope and the bottom of the hull was a flat surface except for the forward end. Ground clearance was estimated to be 26 inches. When first observed, this vehicle was making a 180° change in direction, pivoting on the road on one track.

"Human Torpedo" and One Man Motor Boat.

*88. These two weapons have been used with some success in the Mediterranean by the Italians for attacks on ships in harbour.

(*a*) *Human Torpedo*.—This is a 21-in. torpedo, 22 ft. long, self-propelled by an electric battery, and is fitted with ballast and control water tanks; it is, in fact, a simple type of small submarine. The craft has a detachable explosive head fitted with a time fuze, and has a ram and winch aft.

The crew consists of one officer and one rating, who sit astride the torpedo like jockeys, and are supplied with oxygen apparatus for underwater travel.

The ram and winch are used for lifting the net defence to allow the craft to enter a harbour. The explosive head is detached from the torpedo and fixed as required on the ship to be attacked, the crew retiring on the remaining portion of the craft.

(*b*) *One man motor boat*.—This consists of a small craft, length about 17 ft., with a speed of about 35 knots. The pilot of the boat directs it towards the target and slips off on a wooden raft. The impact of the boat with the target detonates a small charge which splits the boat in two, one part (including the engine) sinking, the other which contains a large charge of T.N.T. exploding below water through the operation of a hydrostatic valve.

Radio Controlled Aerial Torpedoes.

*89. Torpedoes released from aircraft and thence radio controlled have been referred to in several reports; the construction of such projectiles to have a range of 30 km. (18½ miles, *i.e.*, about sufficient to cross the Straits of Dover) is feasible, and the torpedo could probably be made to fly along a radio beam. Errors of range and direction, however, would militate against accurate aiming and would restrict its use at long range to indiscriminate bombing; it might also be employed against shipping. There is no evidence that the project has advanced beyond the experimental stage.

(*b*) *Use of Smoke*

Smoke Battalions and Smoke Regiments.

*90. These are constituted as a separate arm of the service, and are controlled by the Inspectorate of smoke troops and gas defence.

The smoke battalion, which is fully mechanized, consists of headquarters, signals platoon, and three companies, each of which is equipped with eight 10-cm. (3·9-in.) mortars; its peacetime strength was 25 officers and 540 O.Rs.

Its primary function is to lay down smoke-screens, normally covering a front of 1,500 metres (500 metres per company) using a minimum of 4,200 rounds of smoke-shell per hour.

The smoke battalions are trained to fire gas as well as smoke from their mortars, and could, therefore, be used for C.W. at any time.

At least six smoke regiments, each of three smoke battalions, have so far been identified; these units are in the G.H.Q. pool.

In addition to the smoke-shell issued to German artillery, enemy tanks and engineers are both provided with smoke-producing apparatus.

It is possible that, in view of uncertain lines of communication, the Germans would prefer to use the available transport space and weight for lethal (H.E. or gas) ammunition rather than for smoke ammunition. For the same reason the allotment of smoke units might depend upon whether it was intended to use gas or not.

Use by Air Force.

91. Aircraft lay smoke screens in conjunction with operations by land forces, and are likely to do so also when landing troops by parachute or in troop-carrying aircraft. It is believed that special aircraft flying below troop-carrying aircraft sometimes emit a smoke cloud through which parachutists descend and receive protection when most vulnerable.

Smoke in Combined Operations.

92. The landing of troops in this country is likely to be covered by smoke screens if the weather conditions are favourable. In operations inland, limited use of smoke might

be made to cover the crossing and bridging of water obstacles and to conceal the direction of a main attack. Such smoke would probably be produced by aircraft or small generators.

Large Scale Use of Smoke.

93. The employment by the Germans of large scale smoke screens produced by apparatus erected on the Dutch, Belgian or French coasts to cover combined operations against the U.K. must be considered a possibility. No practical experience of such large-scale use of smoke is available, but the possibility of its use cannot be ignored.

It appears to be technically possible in theory for aerial smoke screens to be produced over a target distant up to 100 miles from the point of emission; practically, however, it is unlikely that such screens would be attempted over more than 40-50 miles, and even then they would provide cover from air observation but seldom concealment on land. Technical details on the use of large-scale smoke cloud, *viz.*, its behaviour, vertical and horizontal visibility, rate of emission and suitable meteorological conditions, will be found at Appendix XXIV.

Points of Release.

*94. Suitable points of release could be found anywhere on the Dutch, Belgian or French coasts between the MEUSE Estuary and CHERBOURG. This stretch of coastline, can, for meteorological purposes, be considered in three zones:—

(*a*) Southern North Sea (*i.e.*, coasts of Belgium and Holland) where the limits of suitable wind direction lie between East and South-East.

(*b*) The Straits of Dover, where winds between East and South-West would be suitable.

(*c*) The English Channel, where the wind limits lie between South-East and South-West.

The frequency of suitable meteorological conditions in these zones, with additional notes on special diurnal conditions, is included in Appendix XXIV.

Aircraft and light naval craft would no doubt be available to lay local smoke in the Channel in the normal way, but in addition Siebel Ferries or barges may be specially equipped for this purpose, and each of these craft could probably emit dense smoke for approximately 4 hours or for a longer period, according to the number of units used. Such ferries or barges are likely to proceed with the first flight of invasion craft, and would be moored at intervals in the Channel on flanks of the lines of approach. Arrangements would probably also be made to instal smoke-producing apparatus round the many invasion ports as a measure of defence against bombing attack.

Simultaneous Use of Gas.

95. The possibility of the admixture of toxic gases to the smoke cloud should not be overlooked. This would not in any way affect the screening properties of the cloud.

Tactical Considerations.

96. Some tactical considerations affecting the use of a smoke cloud of the scale referred to are dealt with in para. 130.

(*c*) *Use of Gas*

Resources—General.

*97. (*a*) *Gas.*—The German chemical industry is highly developed and capable of producing large quantities of mustard and phosgene gases; it is known that Germany has already accumulated large supplies of these. Recent reports suggest that her output has been increased and that stocks have been moved from factories to the areas occupied by troops likely to take part in invasion.

(*b*) *Personnel.*—For the use of smoke regiments as C.W. troops, *see* para. 90. Besides the smoke battalions of these regiments, decontamination battalions and road decontamination battalions are known to exist, as independent G.H.Q. units. Their primary purpose is to clear passages through contaminated areas. Their equipment (bulk decontamination vehicles and man-handled sprayers) is equally well adapted to produce contaminations, and they are, therefore, immediately available for offensive C.W.

(*c*) *Weapons.*—The smoke detachments are equipped with 10-cm. mortars and generators, and gas units are reported also to have bulk contamination vehicles, sprayers, chemical mines and projectors. Moreover, artillery, tanks and engineer troops are also equipped with smoke-producing apparatus which could equally well be used for gas.

There is likely, therefore, to be no bar to the use of gas by Germany on account of lack of stocks or of trained personnel or weapons for producing it.

Likelihood of its Use.

98. If Germany attempts to invade this country she will be undertaking a most hazardous operation, and if she considers that the use of gas will increase her chances of success she will not hesitate to use it.

Germany is now well prepared, both as regards the building of gas-proof shelters and the issue of modern gas respirators, to meet any gas attack which may be launched against her. Similar precautions have been taken in occupied countries, particularly along the invasion coasts.

Although thorough anti-gas precautions have been taken by us, and although anti-gas duties form part of our training, the German High Command may think that, if gas is used on the first day of invasion, surprise effect can be obtained, and that the resulting casualties and panic will enable them to gain a firm foothold on these shores.

Types of Gases.

99. The types of gases which are known to be at Germany's disposal include the normal blister, choking, tear and nose gases. Of the blister gases Lewisite, which was being considered by the Germans before the war, needs quicker remedial action than mustard owing to the danger of arsenic systemic poisoning. Experimental work on a wide variety of other gases has been reported from time to time, but it is not thought that any important new war gas has been discovered.

Numerous reports and rumours have been received in the past few months of new unspecified soporific, narcotic, paralysing, numbing and nerve gases. They are all reputed to be without lethal effect, but produce effects which last for periods varying up to some days.

Whilst these reports give the impression of having been deliberately disseminated by the enemy, the possibility of a discovery of such new gas of great potency cannot be entirely excluded.

All such gases at present known, however, require high concentrations to produce incapacitation quickly and, therefore, are not considered practicable for chemical warfare, and are certainly not practicable in connection with invasion by sea or air.

Likely Methods of Use of Gases and Objectives.

100. The most feasible uses of gas by the Germans in an attempted invasion might be as follows:—

(*a*) *Blister gases.* (*Mustard and Lewisite.*)

(i) Spray from aircraft against concentrations of troops or material, *e.g.*, reserves, marching columns and dumps, and against aerodromes and industrial targets.

(ii) Attacks with gas bombs, combined with H.E., delayed action and incendiary bombs, on important communication centres through which our reserves will pass, aerodromes, etc.

(*b*) *Choking gases* (*phosgene, etc.*).

(i) From cylinders mounted on barges, against forward troops.

(ii) From shells or mortar bombs, in conjunction with smoke, against forward troops.

(*c*) *Tear gases.*

Owing to their quick action and silent burst, tear gas grenades are possibly a weapon which will be carried by parachute troops; certain reports tend to confirm this. Tear gases may also be used to disguise other gases.

(*d*) *Nose gases* (*D.A.*, *D.M.*, *D.C.*).

Toxic smokes, used in bombs with a large H.E. burster, may be freely used by dive bombers immediately before an enemy attack. Such bombs are difficult to distinguish from ordinary H.E. bombs. The gas is effective in very low concentrations, and it would provide a quick way of neutralizing opposition, especially in pill boxes which are not gas-proof, and are a difficult target to hit with H.E.

German Gas Tactics.

101. Little is known of the present German doctrine regarding the use of gas. The only guide to the tactics they may employ is the experience of the Great War; as, however, the circumstances attendant on invasion make it impossible to use the same weapons (guns, mortars, etc.) before the attack begins as those then employed, only the principles remain as a guide. From these it would appear possible that Germany might use gas with the following objects:—

(*a*) *Against military objectives.*

(i) To isolate a sector of attack by continuous belts of persistent gas.

This would require so many aircraft to be used for so long before invasion that it would be uneconomical and would forfeit surprise. It cannot, therefore, be considered a likely object.

(ii) To cause delay-action casualties among reserves by bombing and spraying centres of communication.

While this would be feasible with the resources available it is doubtful if it would be sufficiently effective to warrant the expenditure of material and effort involved.

(iii) To gain air superiority by attacking aerodromes with H.E. and a combination of gas spray and gas bombs.

This is considered a probable objective.

(iv) To mislead by putting down a harmless persistent gas, resembling mustard, in the sector chosen for attack.

This would not be successful if troops are thoroughly trained in the recognition of gases and expert analysts are quickly available.

(v) To put forward troops out of action.

The enemy might hope to achieve this by the liberal use of lethal gases and toxic smokes, relying on surprise effect to attain his object.

(*b*) *Against industry and civilians.*

To cause general confusion by dropping H.E., gas and incendiary bombs on industrial undertakings, docks and civilians.

Although this might be worth while if, owing to lack of protective measures, the effect on morale were serious, knowledge of the enemy suggests that he will not disperse his air-borne gas effort on civilians generally. He may, however, use gas to cause panic among civilian refugees on the front of his advance with the object of blocking the roads in the track of our counter attacks.

Scale of Gas Attack from the Air.

102. The scale of gas attack from the air might be as follows:—

(*a*) At maximum effort, the Germans might for two or three days maintain some 2,500 sorties per day, all of which might involve gas; but the total load of gas carried is unlikely to exceed 50 per cent. of the total offensive load. This amounts to 2,500 tons of gas per day *as a maximum*.

(*b*) At sustained effort a maximum of 880 sorties per day may be expected (for a period not exceeding a month), in which all aircraft might carry gas. The gas load would be unlikely to exceed 50 per cent. of the total offensive load (*i.e.*, 880 tons of gas per day *as a maximum*).

Effect of Wind.

103. (*a*) Light favourable winds of 4-12 miles per hour are essential for the release of gas clouds from the sea. (*See* Appendix XXIV, paras. 5-7.)

(*b*) With experienced pilots the effect of wind on aircraft spray is negligible.

(*c*) Whilst gas bombs are most effective under conditions of calm or light winds, the initial effects in close proximity to the bomb-burst will be considerable even with a strong wind, although the period will be lessened during which the air in the vicinity remains dangerous.

(*d*) *Use of A.A.*

" Battle Ferries ".

*104. Considerable information is available regarding the types of A.A. guns and craft to be employed.

The special use of heavy and light A.A. guns on Siebel ferries is dealt with in detail in paras. 47-48 and in Appendix XI.

Floating A.A. Defence.

105. There have been several references to A.A. on barges, including one to barges of about 500 tons on which L.A.A. and M.G. emplacements were being prepared.

Normally there are some fifty 2-cm. (·79-in.), nine 3·7-cm. (1·45-in.) and twelve 8·8-cm. (3·46-in.) A.A. guns operating with an armoured division, but it is not known what additional provision would be made for floating A.A. defence.

The types of A.A. gun which could be used are the following:—

(*a*) *Barges*:—2·0-cm (·79-in.) (effective ceiling 6,500 ft.); the 3·7-cm. (1·45-in.) (12,000 ft.) would be the heaviest possible and would involve suitable structural strengthening of the barge.

(*b*) Danish and other train ferries:—2·0-cm. (·79-in.), 3·7-cm. (1·45-in.), 4·7-cm. (1·85-in.) (17,000 ft.) and possibly 7·5-cm. (2·95-in.) (approx. 30,000 ft.) with suitable strengthening.

(*c*) Vessels of 1,000 tons and over:—as for ferries, but two 8·8-cm. (3·46-in.) guns (approx. 34,000 ft.) could probably be mounted in ships of this size suitably strengthened; draught of these would be about 10 ft.

Methods of Employment.

106. The method of employment envisaged by the Germans is not known, but the following are possibilities:—

(*a*) In the case of a ship landing, A.A. protection would probably be provided from larger vessels, either naval or merchant vessels.

(*b*) In large-scale landings, A.A. as in para. 105 (*a*) would be provided in addition to naval A.A.; Siebel ferries would probably be employed also.

(*c*) As many barges have been adapted to allow rapid disembarkation of guns and vehicles, A.A. guns could be similarly disembarked and in this case their normal mobile mountings would be used. The German A.A. gun is an all-purpose weapon and could be used against concrete works and A.F.Vs. The 8·8-cm. is well supplied with A.P. ammunition.

PART V

Possible Enemy Strategy and Tactics

General Principles.

107. The fundamental principles regarding German strategy, tactics and methods of warfare as they apply to possible operations against the U.K. are clear and well defined, and may be summarized under the following headings:—

(*a*) *The use of overwhelming numbers to obtain surprise.*

Germany has forfeited strategical surprise in the invasion of Great Britain, but she can still obtain tactical surprise by the use of overwhelming numbers.

(*b*) *Attacks on a wide front.*

These may be made with the object of inducing the defender to disperse his forces, and to deceive him as to the true point of attack; attacks may range from Iceland along the East and South coasts of Great Britain to Ireland.

(*c*) *Speed and ruthlessness in the execution of the plan.*

These are cardinal principles in German strategical teaching, and have been well demonstrated in previous campaigns. There will be no hesitation in using, even against civilians, gas or other methods of warfare if thought advantageous.

(*d*) *Thorough training and experience, especially in handling mechanized formations.*

Campaigns in Poland, Norway, the West and Russia have given German commanders and all ranks invaluable experience of active operations, and the Germans may, therefore, carry out strategical and tactical moves which might well appear impossible.

(*e*) *Low flying air attack.*

This has been one of the most successful German methods against troops and civilians.

(*f*) *Appropriate means to achieve a given object.*

The German Army has always produced the type of troops and equipment required for a specific object, and it must be assumed that for the invasion of the U.K. she has built special landing craft, evolved means of dealing with beach fortifications and envisaged arrangements for supply and maintenance of her forces.

(*g*) *Exploitation of undue optimism in their enemy.*

The Germans have in previous campaigns in this war taken full advantage of adversaries who have overestimated their own strength.

(*h*) *Alarm and confusion in the civil population.*

This was one of the principal sources of success in the Western Campaign; as all communications may be cut on invasion, it is essential that the civil population should know what, and what not, to do.

(*j*) *Exploitation of disgruntled minorities.*

The Germans are likely to make use of certain Irish elements in a manner similar to that made of minorities in Poland, Belgium, etc.

(*k*) *Attempts to weaken morale of civil population and fighting forces.*

The enemy has not attempted to attack a population when its morale was high, and will therefore make every endeavour before invading to lower morale by bombing, blockade and propaganda.

(*l*) *Choice of unexpected course of action.*

The saying that "If there are three courses of action open to the enemy he will choose the fourth" is particularly applicable to German methods and has already been put into practice on several well-known occasions in the present war.

(*m*) *Concentration of effort.*

The Germans put as much power into the main effort and as little power into the subsidiary effort as possible. Early distinction by Intelligence Staffs between the former and the latter is of extreme importance.

(*n*) *Co-operation between the various arms and services.*

Particular stress is laid upon the closest co-operation between the various arms and between the various services themselves; in particular, the co-operation between the G.A.F. and armoured formations has been one of the outstanding features of German operations.

Surprise.

108. German training concentrates on speed and surprise, the utilization of a favourable situation, and above all on the importance of boldness and decision. Surprise on a short sea crossing, where the trip can be completed on one night, is always a possibility, but in the case of a longer journey, complete surprise should be impossible, unless distant reconnaissance were impeded by bad weather.

The use of smoke, gas and surprise tactics and ruses of every kind (*e.g.*, the use of British uniforms), is to be expected. Attempts will be made to secure surprise by the intensity and scale of air attacks rather than by other means, although naturally everything possible will be done to keep secret the date of the attack.

Areas of Attack.

109. The need for providing their main attack with the maximum degree of fighter cover (for the radii of action of German aircraft *see* Appendix XIX), the limited seaworthiness of the many small craft involved, the desire to simplify as far as possible the problem of the protection of convoys en route, and the difficulties of subsequent maintenance by long sea crossings, will probably restrict the extent of the *main* German attack to the area between the WASH and WEYMOUTH.

A means by which this front could be satisfactorily extended would be by the prior capture of aerodromes in S.E. England or East Anglia with the particular object of securing fighter cover over the English North-East ports. Protection and maintenance of these aerodromes, however, would hardly be practicable in the face of British air attacks.

Scale of Attack.

*110. Having once decided upon invasion the Germans will undoubtedly concentrate the maximum possible effort, and will be prepared to accept very heavy casualties.

The main factors in assessing the scale of attack are the following:—

(*a*) The number of formations which the enemy can land, having regard both to off-shore conditions (*e.g.*, currents, shoals, etc.), and to the extent and suitability of beaches.

(*b*) The size and importance of the area in which the main attack is to take place.

(*c*) The availability of suitable craft, *i.e.* M/Vs., barges, etc.

(*d*) The size of convoys in relation to the areas in which they must assemble, and routes to be traversed.

At Appendix XXV will be found a statement of the coastal categories in United Kingdom and Northern Ireland, showing the total mileage of coastline, length of coastline suitable for landing armoured formations and for other arms respectively. The gradients of beaches have an important bearing upon the unloading from T.L.Cs. and barges of tanks and other vehicles; the Appendix referred to includes, therefore, a note on the draught of German T.L.Cs., etc., and the water fording capacity of German A.F.Vs. and M.T.

A detailed table of the beach gradients between the WASH and WEYMOUTH will be found at Appendix XXVI.

The scale of attack included in the first edition of "Notes on Invasion" is not reproduced in the present edition in view of the constantly changing factors which may affect it (*e.g.*, changes in German strength, both military and air, improvements in invasion craft and technique, etc.) and of the consequent danger of misleading commanders of troops defending specific areas.

The matter is kept constantly under review and relevant information on which commanders can base their estimates and dispositions will be circulated through normal Intelligence channels.

Diversions.

*111. The reasons for assuming that the main attack upon the United Kingdom must be in S.E. England are given in para. 109. Diversionary attacks are only likely to be made where they impose a greater reduction on the strength of the defence than in that of the attackers. The British forces which the enemy is most likely to consider in this respect are light naval forces, fighters, bombers, armoured divisions, and mobile divisions, and the value of diversions must depend mainly on the effect achieved on these forces.

The enemy's best chance of concealment and surprise lies in carrying out the whole movement from port of embarkation to point of attack during darkness. 6-knot barges are too slow to make any but a short passage in darkness; merchant ships, train ferries and passenger ships would have the necessary speed but, in order to discharge vehicles and stores, would have to remain anchored off-shore for a considerable period of daylight during which they would suffer heavy losses if seriously attacked from the sea or air.

Enemy naval or air forces could probably not be spared from the area of main attack in sufficient strength to protect shipping in this situation. The enemy would thus be dependent upon having sufficient T.C.Ls., which are the most suitable craft for this purpose; at 12 knots they could, in April, make the passage to any part of the coast south of the line Cromer to Land's End entirely under cover of darkness.

In view of these considerations practically the whole of a diversionary force would have to make the passage simultaneously and would have to be organized to gain a bridgehead rapidly; it would need fighter cover during any passage at sea in daylight, during its attack on the beaches and during disembarkation. Its subsequent supply and maintenance would depend on single ships, which might be able to run in under cover or darkness, supplemented by air-borne supply. The original expedition would need to take with it supplies and reserves for about a fortnight.

*112. In addition to diversions on parts of the coast of the United Kingdom other than S.E., the following are possibilities:—

Eire.
Iceland (C).
Faroes.
Orkneys.
Scotland.
Northern Ireland.

Attacks on any part of the coast of the United Kingdom made as diversions from the main attack in the S.E. would have a common characteristic, *viz.*: their success in diverting British forces from the main area would last only as long as the forces landed, or to be landed, constituted in the view of the defenders an important threat; forces so small as easily to be overwhelmed or so immobile as to be incapable of operating more than a few miles inland could not constitute an important threat.

*113. One of the most likely areas for such an attack would be East Anglia, which would be suitable as part of a pincer movement on London and as an area containing a number of important aerodromes.

Attacks in Dorset and Lincolnshire would also offer many advantages, and the enemy might consider the possibility of capturing some small British port relatively distant from the main attack in order to disembark forces from M.Vs., *i.e.*, without drawing upon his restricted resources in T.L.Cs.

An attack on the East Coast of Scotland might have some moral rather than material value, and an expedition in passenger and merchant ships might be prepared in Norwegian ports. In view of the obvious hazards of the crossing, its actual despatch would probably be dependent upon events in other sectors. A possible diversion against Eire is dealt with in para. 129.

Roles of Airborne Troops.

*114. Airborne troops might be used against this country either:—

(*a*) with the object of attacking and sabotaging key points, such as aircraft and other important factories engaged in war production, concentrations of aircraft (*e.g.*, in reserve parks), communications and public utilities, with the object of crippling our war effort; or

(*b*) as an integral part of invasion.

Air-borne attack on a large scale must, however, to be effective, be followed up, within a very few days at most, by a successful sea-borne invasion; otherwise the air-borne troops, though they would create a great deal of damage and dislocation, in a short time would inevitably be overwhelmed.

The first object would not be expected to have a conclusive effect on our power to continue the war, and therefore could only be regarded as of long-term value. While precautions against this method of employing airborne troops cannot be relaxed, it is thought unlikely that it would be attempted, apart possibly from isolated raids, unless the Germans had abandoned all hope of invasion.

The question of airborne attacks directed against our fighter aerodromes is developed more fully below (*vide* para. 117).

Probable Employment of Airborne Troops.

*115. Any German airborne forces taking part in attempted invasion of this country will be subordinated to the role of enabling substantial military forces to obtain a bridge-head which can be exploited; this is likely to include the capture of landing grounds. It is considered, therefore, that the enemy would be unlikely to disperse his effort, which is necessarily limited by availability of aircraft, and that he would concentrate it in the area where the main bridge-head or bridge-heads are to be established. Any dispersal of effort would be on a small scale solely by way of diversion, unless unexpected success enabled the Germans to exploit it. The German High Command probably think that this country, both by character and by organization, including the Home Guard, would deal promptly and effectively with isolated bodies of parachute troops.

Other ways in which the Germans could employ airborne troops to assist their invasion plans are likely to include:—

(*a*) crippling our fighter defences by widespread surprise attacks against fighter aerodromes in South-East and Southern England, or

(*b*) *major* diversions in areas far from the main landings, *e.g.*, in Southern Ireland, Scotland or South-West England.

(*c*) (i) the destruction or neutralization of the British R.D.F. chain.

(ii) the destruction of Control Centres, Operation Rooms, etc.

(iii) the dislocation of communications.

(iv) the assassination of senior officers.

The cumulative effect of these attacks would be important and would probably form part of any general plan of invasion, even though it would not have the effect of neutralizing the R.A.F. for a prolonged period.

In a densely populated country such as this the Germans would no doubt attempt to hamper military movements by disorganization of the civilian population outside the main areas of attack. For this purpose bombing, gas attacks and fifth column activities are more likely to be employed than air-landings.

The German High Command would not attempt invasion of this country unless they were prepared to press operations ruthlessly home with the supreme object of ending the war; they would be unlikely, therefore, to be deterred from using the whole of their available resources by such considerations as conserving resources for the future.

Operations in other theatres of war would, for the time being, be reduced to a minimum. If and so far as they were continued they would be merely by way of diversions.

Weather has obviously a bearing on air operations. Successful invasion, however, must in the last analysis depend upon the ability of the German High Command to effect the passage and subsequent maintenance of seaborne troops. It is probable, therefore, that weather conditions affecting transit by sea are likely to be the governing factor in selection of the time for invasion.

Principal Objectives in the Bridgehead area.

*116. The bulk of the airborne forces is likely, as indicated above, to be employed against the area or areas selected by the Germans for establishment of the main bridgeheads. It is considered that the Germans must obtain their main bridgehead in South-East England, where fighter cover can be afforded and supplies be subsequently maintained by the shortest sea route, also capable of being covered by fighters (*vide* para. 109). The particular objectives to establish the bridgehead, in order of priority, are thought to be as follows:—

(*a*) The capture of territory necessary for establishing the main bridgehead or bridgeheads, which would necessitate the capture of flat ground or beaches where troop-carrying aircraft could land in force. The main areas chosen are likely to be the coastal belts (up to some 20 miles inland) of South-East England and of East Anglia.

The immediate objectives of attack in these areas are likely to be convenient aerodromes (especially fighter) in the vicinity, open stretches of country (such as downland), and suitable beaches.

(*b*) The landing of parachute troops at nodal points on approaches to the captured aerodromes, to prevent interference by counter-attack with their use by the Germans.

(*c*) The capture of positions immediately in rear of our forward defences.

(*d*) The capture of important communication points immediately in rear of the main landing areas to hamper the arrival of reinforcements.

(*e*) The capture of approaches to ports.

(*f*) The capture of other fighter aerodromes over an extended area in South-East England after hold over those in the immediate vicinity of the main landing areas has been established.

(*g*) The putting out of action of R.D.F. stations, thereby further weakening our fighter defences. These are likely to be the objects of low bombing and fighter attacks, but to ensure the destruction of stations in the vicinity of the main landings, small parties of parachutists might be dropped.

(*h*) The putting out of action of important headquarters, such as Fighter Command. Bombing is the most probable method of attack on these, but the possibility of small parachute " damage and surrender " raids cannot be entirely excluded.

(*j*) The seizure of important road, rail and telephonic junctions, *e.g.*, ASHFORD, CANTERBURY and MAIDSTONE, to create confusion and cause interference in rear of the main area of battle.

Airborne Attacks on Fighter Aerodromes.

*117. As the attempt to cripple our fighter defences by combat in the air and by the bombing of aerodromes proved a failure in August and September, 1940, the Germans must, as an essential part of or preliminary to invasion, devise some other means for substantially reducing the power of our fighter defences; these might take the form of surprise attacks (including possibly the use of gas spray) against a large number of key fighter aerodromes and sector headquarters by airborne troops. The Germans might be willing to sacrifice as much as one half of their available transport aircraft to achieve this.

Any aerodromes and landing grounds suitable for airborne landings in and around the areas where the main bridgeheads are to be established will be primary objectives of any airborne attack.

The object of such attacks would probably be to put aircraft at dispersal points out of action by light automatic or mortar fire or grenades rather than to attempt to put aerodromes out of action. Parachutists with " homing " beacons might be dropped the previous night in order to guide the aircraft bearing the assaulting infantry. The use of light airborne tanks in such an operation is also a possibility.

Limiting Factors.

*118. The German High Command must, in considering any plan for attacking our fighter resources take into account the following factors, most of which will be known to them and the remainder of which must be surmised:—

(*a*) The total transport aircraft believed to be available to the Germans is limited to some 1,200 operationally effective. The loss of a substantial part of this force would be felt when attempts were being made to establish bridgeheads.

(*b*) If such an attack against our fighter aerodromes is to be a prelude to invasion it must be followed up immediately by a seaborne expedition. The preparations for this would have to be on such a large scale that they would certainly become known to us, thereby eliminating the factor of strategical surprise.

(*c*) Even the concentration of a large proportion of the German transport aircraft in areas from which this country could be reached without our receiving at least 24 hours' warning is highly improbable.

(*d*) With such warning our forces, including Fighter Command, would be operating under a state of alert, so that fighter aircraft and crews would be ready to take off at the shortest possible notice. The Germans would assume that plans had been made for dispersal of fighter aircraft over a considerable number of aerodromes, and possibly for abandonment of the more vulnerable aerodromes near the coast.

(*e*) During their attacks in the Autumn of 1940 the German High Command must have realized that our fighter defences are organized in depth and that the neutralizing of a few fighter aerodromes would not be sufficient to prevent the continued operation of the fighter defences as a whole. They would probably envisage, therefore, the necessity of attacking simultaneously upwards of 40 aerodromes.

Air Attack on London.

*119. The Germans might attempt to capture the seat of government in London by air-borne attack. To have reasonable chance of success this would involve almost the whole of the enemy's airborne effort, and would be most difficult owing to the limited landing areas, the difficulties of transportation, the presence of the Home Guard, and the need for pilots really experienced in this work. It is considered that the enemy would thus prejudice the success of his seaborne invasion by withdrawing from it the air-borne support that might be essential for initial success. If dislocation at the moment of invasion were his main object, he might hope to achieve this by intensive air bombardment, possibly coupled with the use of gas.

If, on the other hand, the enemy were willing to accept these risks and difficulties, and achieved even partial success, a major airborne attack might well cause more serious dislocation than would intensive air bombardment, even if accompanied by the large scale use of gas.

Tactics of Airborne Troops.

*120. The distance from departure aerodromes (or Rear H.Q.) to the scene of operations in CRETE was approximately the same as in the attack on HOLLAND, *i.e.*, about 200 miles. If the departure aerodromes are too near to the objective, they may be discovered in advance; concentrations of transport planes are conspicuous, and the advantages of surprise will be forfeited, even if the force is not, as is likely to happen, destroyed before it starts. On the other hand, there are many reasons why the distance from Rear H.Q. to objective should not be great:—

- (*a*) If fighter support is to be provided, the range must be restricted accordingly.
- (*b*) Over longer distances, more aircraft are needed to maintain ferrying capacity.
- (*c*) Over longer distances, decisions taken at the rear take progressively longer to affect the action.
- (*d*) Troops going into action should not be kept too long seated in aircraft.
- (*e*) In general, the operation becomes progressively more difficult for pilots over longer distances.

*121. The Germans are likely to subject the areas where landings by airborne troops are intended, to a short but intensive preliminary low-level bombing or machine-gun attack against such objectives as A.A. guns, aerodrome defences and troop positions. In CRETE, where ground forces had no fighter cover, casualties directly attributable to dive bombing attacks were comparatively low when troops were dispersed and dug in, although these attacks greatly hampered movement of the defending forces by day. This bombing will cease in the landing areas so soon as the airborne troops start to arrive, but is likely to be continued all round the objective.

The air bombardment is likely to be followed up by an airborne attack which may take the following form:—

(*a*) A preliminary wave of shock troops (probably in part glider-borne) with the task of neutralizing A.A. defences and dislocating communications.

(*b*) Following immediately on this, large descents of parachute troops, with the task of seizing a landing ground; these descents will probably be at several points 15 miles or so apart.

(*c*) Later, possibly by several hours, strong reinforcements of parachute troops in those areas where the first wave has been successful, followed by troops in transport aircraft.

(*d*) Air-landing troops, theoretically as soon as landing ground is prepared, but in case of necessity even earlier.

*122. Normally, the shock-troops will work by companies. They will be instructed to get in touch with neighbouring units, probably battalions or regiments, as soon as possible. After accomplishing their initial task, they will be instructed to join up with and take orders from the higher formations which have subsequently descended. For this, wireless communications will be essential.

Main bodies of parachute troops will be instructed to attack their objective, probably an aerodrome, *as a co-ordinated unit or formation*. Before an attack of any importance is launched, companies will get into contact with battalions, and battalions with regiments. Companies may descend some distance apart (say ½ mile to 1½ miles), but they will try to land so that they can operate as a normal infantry unit. To produce the requisite co-ordination, wireless communication will be essential from the moment the descent is complete. The area covered by one main attacking body may be as much as eight miles by three miles.

In addition to the equipment mentioned in Appendix XX, arms carried on the person of parachutists landing in CRETE were an automatic pistol, four hand grenades, and a large knife; in the first platoons to land one man in four carried a Tommy gun. All other weapons were carried in separately dropped containers which had to be located and opened, a process occupying several minutes.

In CRETE the density at which parachute troops landed on the first day was from 400 to 500 parachutists per square mile; the average height at which parachutists are released from the aircraft is 300 to 400 feet, the aircraft travelling at about 100 m.p.h.

The parachutists' first task is to collect weapons and munitions dropped separately by parachute. In CRETE those who landed in areas occupied by our troops had such heavy casualties that their inclination was to hide and take no active part in proceedings for several hours. Experience showed that parachutists were most vulnerable within 10 to 15 minutes after they had landed, but if they were given time to collect in organized bodies they recovered their morale. Their aim will be to bring into action mortars and heavy machine guns which were very accurate and effective in CRETE. The Germans will have learnt their lesson that it is disastrous to drop parachutists actually among the defending troops.

Parachutists are, therefore, likely to be dropped in depth round any aerodromes or areas selected for attack, instead of being concentrated on the site itself.

*123. Although it is known that in CRETE the landing of troops by aircraft did not take place until the day following the initial parachute attack, it is thought that the Germans would, in face of our air fighter defences, mobile reserves and organized land defences, be compelled to reinforce their parachute troops at the earliest moment or fail for certain. Light artillery and tracked motor-cycles were landed in troop-carrying aircraft.

The use of smoke laid by aircraft in the actual dropping zone of parachute troops is considered unlikely. Parachute troops are, however, well equipped to make tactical use of smoke on the ground. They also may carry a few tear gas bombs.

It is not known how light A.F.Vs., if brought, would be employed. On the other hand, the anti-tank equipment of all types of airborne troops is, as it must be, considerable.

As in all German operations, an airborne attack will be based on, and is particularly suited to, the principle of *reinforcing success*. The initial plan will be only a short-term one, the later stages depending entirely on reports of initial successes being received at H.Q.

*124. No evidence exists of direct wireless communication between troops in action and supporting aircraft. Supplies and bomber-support will probably be demanded by means of flags, ground-strips and flares. Fighter support will be demanded by wireless communication through the normal channels back to Rear H.Q.

No airborne operations have yet been carried out by night. A descent on a moonlight night is considered possible, but the difficulty with which detachments would be confronted in accurately determining their position might cause them to defer any attack until dawn, in which case tactics would be similar to those following a daylight descent. A descent on a very dark night is unlikely.

In view of the losses incurred in making airborne attacks in Crete by day, it is possible that attacks in areas involving fairly deep penetration behind coastal areas would be made by moonlight. While a rather higher rate of casualties, due to accidents on land, would be incurred, loss from fighters and ground fire would be less heavy. A large proportion of the landings might go unnoticed and the troops would have a longer period in which to sort themselves out before going into action. Properly trained airborne troops landed by moonlight should be able to join up with others dropped from the same aircraft and with their weapons, although less quickly than by day. As, however, it would take them some hours to locate themselves, make contact with other parties and find their way to their objectives, they would probably be dropped early in the night.

Airborne troops will depend more than ordinary infantry on the use of wireless, at least until they have overcome any immediate opposition and have become a co-ordinated force. Thereafter they will act as ordinary infantry and will be less dependent on wireless communication except for traffic with their Rear H.Q.

If, as may well be the case, there is any organization for the dropping of small parties or parachutists as "saboteurs" in the proper sense, with or without disguises, no use has yet been made of them. At least it would be quite distinct in its methods and objectives from the regular parachute infantry of XI Air Corps. (*See* paras. 66-69.)

Embarkation and Transport.

125. The enemy's problem of the provision of transport for the sea crossing divides itself into two main items:—

(*a*) the provision of transport for the "short crossing" from N.W. EUROPE, *i.e.*, from the coast between approximately FLUSHING and LE HAVRE;

(*b*) the provision of transport for the "long crossing" from SCANDINAVIA, N. GERMANY and the West Coast of FRANCE.

The main differences between the two problems lie in the form of shipping required and the time taken to cross. In the former, barges and shallow-draught craft can be used with safety in suitable sea conditions, and the crossing, from the point of view of distance only, can be completed during the hours of darkness. In the latter, shallow-draught craft would not be practicable, nor could the crossing be completed in one night.

*126. The distance between various invasion ports and the nearest points in the British Isles, together with the approximate time and passage at varying speeds is given in Appendix XXVII; a map of the coastline of North-West EUROPE showing the invasion ports is at Appendix XXVIII.

Appendix XXIX shows a possible distribution in Channel ports of invasion craft, based on:—

(*a*) the capacity of the ports most conveniently situated for an attack on South-East England and East Anglia;

(*b*) the craft which the enemy may have available by May, 1942, if operations against the U.K. are intended (*see* Appendix IV, Table 2).

*127. A brief account of recent enemy activity in the chief invasion ports is given at Appendix XXX; particulars of the extent to which the more northerly ports are likely to be effected by ice conditions are given in Appendix XXXI.

128. The area of sea likely to be covered by invasion craft is as follows:—

(*a*) an armoured division carried in about 250 barges would probably sail in groups of about 25 (1 mile by 1 mile) at 3-mile (½-hour) intervals;

(*b*) an infantry division carried in some 10 merchant vessels and 50 barges would occupy an area about 1 mile wide by 1½ miles deep.

EIRE.

*129. Special considerations apply to the possibility of operations against Eire. These might be specially attractive to the enemy on account of the value of Eire as a base for operations against the U.K.; the facts that the Germans can probably rely on considerable help both from Fifth Column and from I.R.A., and that they are moreover well served from the intelligence point of view by their diplomatic representatives resident in Eire, must be considered additional incentives to undertake an attack upon that country. Despite the numerous reports received from time to time of German intention to attack Eire, it is not thought likely that this would be undertaken except as part of a full scale attack against the U.K. The difficulties of maintaining a seaborne force make a separate operation unlikely, and despite the success attained by the Germans in Crete it is unlikely that they would rate highly their chances of obtaining a similar success in Eire, chiefly because of the size of the force which it would be necessary to transport and maintain by air; R.A.F. fighter defences could moreover be made available within a very short period even if they were not available at the actual time of invasion.

In relation to the Battle of the Atlantic the attack on Eire has important possibilities from the enemy point of view, in so far as a threat upon Eire would necessitate British naval forces being held ready to deal with such an attack. On these grounds it is possible that the enemy might prepare a force with its shipping and hold it in Atlantic ports either as a threat only or, by actually attacking Eire, to divert British forces from England.

Whilst a diversion to Northern Ireland may come from Norwegian or Baltic ports, any main attack might also come from these ports, but is more likely, in order to avoid the hazards of a long North Sea crossing, to come from the French Atlantic Coast, *e.g.,* BORDEAUX where ample loading and berthing accommodation is available.

The ports in Eire which the enemy might attempt to use are referred to in Appendix XXXV.

Cover for Landing.

130. The best cover for landings is probably the indistinct light of dawn or the use of mist or smoke. The possibility of smoke on a large scale has already been referred to (*vide* paras. 93-96), but it should be realised that navigation in such a cloud would be even more difficult

than at night and would be liable to hinder the invading force and its supporting aircraft almost as much as it would help, unless the special radio devices for accurate navigation in fog prove to be very efficient. If smoke is to be used it is more likely that it would be produced from low-flying aircraft either by smoke candles dropped on the beaches, by a smoke curtain released from the aircraft itself, or by mortar-fire from small craft.

In any case, it must be recognized that an attacking force using smoke on a large scale can only expect one of two possibilities, viz.:—

(*a*) the screen will remain down, in which case it will not seriously affect aircraft movement; or

(*b*) the screen will rise, in which case surface craft will not be greatly affected.

131. Offensive cover for a landing can be expected to take the form of:—

(*a*) Attack by dive bombers to destroy or neutralize located defences.

(*b*) The use of grounded barges, heavily protected with steel or concrete and armed with M.Gs., anti-tank guns, field guns and flame throwers. The use of such "barge pillboxes", together with the co-operation of dive-bombers, would, to a certain extent, overcome the normal lack of artillery support for landings. Naval guns are an unsatisfactory solution to the problem owing to their flat trajectory and difficulties of communication and observation. Considerable use would probably be made of Siebel ferries.

(*c*) The disembarkation of A.F.Vs. in the first flight ashore.

(*d*) The use of gas in the form of cloud, spray or bomb.

(*e*) Anchored craft containing A.A. guns and apparatus for a balloon barrage.

(*f*) Parachutists and airborne forces landed in rear of the beach defences.

Removal of Obstacles.

132. (*a*) *Offshore.*—Such obstacles consist mainly of mines. The defenders' mine-fields can be swept unless covered by artillery fire, naval forces, or strong aircraft

patrols. The Germans' own mine-fields, which might otherwise prove a liability, can be laid with a self-destroying device so that they are no longer effective after a certain date.

(*b*) *Inshore*.—There is a variety of inshore obstacles which might be used. The following are possible means for attempting to overcome them:—

(i) Craft carrying powerful explosives driven on to the obstructions, evacuated, and fired by time fuze.

(ii) Craft with reinforced bottoms used to charge obstacles at a period about high tide.

(iii) Depth charge or torpedoes fired by motor boats.

(*c*) *Beach obstacles*.—These are similar to normal land anti-tank and anti-personnel obstacles and would probably be dealt with by similar methods. It is probable, therefore, that wire would be attacked by means of bangalore torpedoes or remote-controlled land torpedoes, either of which would also have the effect of clearing mines in the vicinity. Wire can also be scaled by means of special ramps. Concrete obstacles would be attacked by anti-tank or anti-aircraft guns and by guns mounted on A.F.Vs., or by special charges placed by engineer assault troops under cover of fire. Minefields would be cleared as mentioned above either by bangalore or remote-controlled torpedo, by engineer detachments using explosive nets or, under cover of darkness or smoke, removing the mines by hand. Any of the obstacles mentioned might also be cleared in advance of the attack by dive-bombing attacks or by rocket barrage, or by M.G. and mortar fire from small craft.

Employment of Guns Against Concrete Defences.

*133. A list of the guns with which German field formations used for invasion of this country are likely to be equipped is given at Appendix XXXII.

The special types of heavy guns and howitzers whose sole rôle is to destroy heavily fortified positions have not been considered; if the Germans think it necessary to employ such types there is no doubt that they will make special arrangements to do so.

The following weapons in these tables deserve particular attention:—

M.G. 34.—This machine gun which is standard equipment in all types of divisions and in all A.F.Vs. can, in certain circumstances, be expected to fire solely A.P. and

A.P. tracer ammunition. The penetration of this type of ammunition will of course greatly exceed that which is possible with normal ammunition.

2-*cm.* (·79-*in.*) *A.A.*/*A.Tk. Gun* (2-*cm. Flak* 30).—This gun can be expected in very large numbers and in a variety of forms, *viz.*, on ordinary mobile mounting, on self propelled mounting, on armoured cars, carriers, light tanks and shallow-draft craft.

8·8-*cm.* (3·46-*in.*) *Flak* 18.—This is the most effective German A.Tk. weapon. Platoons may be allotted to infantry divs. It can be expected not only on its normal field and self-propelled mountings, but will probably also be used from special shallow-draft sea going carrier craft (*vide* paras. 47 and 48). There is evidence to suggest that it is in this form intended, whilst afloat, for the attack on land targets.

10·5-*cm.* (4·14-*in.*) *LFH* 18.—This gun howitzer has been involved in actions against Russian tanks, and it can be expected as an anti-concrete weapon firing A.P. shells with base fuze.

*134. Guns to be used against concrete may be employed by:—

(*a*) seaborne troops landed on beaches.

(*b*) airborne troops.

(*c*) close support assault craft.

(*d*) tanks either ashore or in T.L.Cs.

Any of the guns shown in Appendix XXXII may be landed on the beaches or mounted in special types of close support assault craft.

Those guns marked "T" in this Appendix may be mounted in tanks which could be landed on the beaches from T.L.Cs. or barges, and those marked "A" can be brought by airborne troops.

Though the penetration for a number of these guns against armoured plate is known, their penetration of ferro-concrete is not known; there is, in any case, no standard unit of "toughness" of ferro-concrete. For those German guns whose penetrative performances are not known, fair estimates could be made by comparing them with British guns of nearly similar calibre and muzzle velocity, firing the same type of ammunition.

Mechanized Reconnaissance Units.

135. In operations in the United Kingdom these units would be likely to be among the first landed. They will probably strike inland as far and as fast as possible, relying on seizing supplies of petrol and food. They are likely to operate in small patrols consisting of armoured cars, motor-cyclists and possibly a few light tanks.

136. The object of mechanized reconnaissance units may be:—

(*a*) To reconnoitre and report the location and strength of British forces.

(*b*) While avoiding combat with large forces or strongly defended localities, to over-run small centres of resistance which would impede the advance of the main forces.

(*c*) To prevent the carrying out of demolitions and to disrupt communications, *e.g.*, telephone exchanges, wireless stations, etc.

(*d*) To establish contact with parachute and other air-borne troops already landed.

(*e*) By rapid movement and indiscriminate firing to give the impression of the presence of large forces. One object will be to create panic and confusion and to get refugees crowding the roads.

They may also be employed to seize and hold covering positions or bridgeheads, and to protect troops or material which are being landed. During the advance inland, mechanized reconnaissance units may be given the task of holding an exposed flank covering demolitions prepared by their engineer detachments.

Armoured Formations.

137. In the U.K. armoured formations may be expected to avoid those districts where the country is much enclosed. Elsewhere they will take advantage of the abundance of good roads and attempt to overrun large areas, where possible using infiltration tactics, *i.e.*, finding a way round rather than attacking obstacles strongly held. When they are obliged to attack, medium and light tanks will co-operate closely and where necessary will call on artillery or dive-bombing aircraft to assist them in overcoming opposition. In wooded country lorried infantry may be employed to clear paths for tanks.

Villages which have been organized as strong points and have been provided with anti-tank defences are likely to be attacked by dive-bombers using incendiary bombs. Similar tactics are likely to be used against tank blocks in villages if the tanks fail to overcome resistance with their own resources. When tank blocks are encountered, light tanks are likely to give way to the medium; their tactics will be to fire into the obstacles and in some cases to use incendiary hand grenades against them. As anti-tank guns are often sited to give flanking fire, German A.F.Vs. will attempt to engage them frontally before the guns can face a new direction.

Motorized Infantry and Infantry Divisions.

138. Motorized divisions are organized on the same general lines as infantry divisions; they are, however, on a two infantry regiment basis, have a lower establishment in artillery, and all their units are mechanized throughout.

Infantry divisions normally have a high proportion of horse drawn transport, but it is believed that for operations against the U.K. they also will have mechanized transport, and possibly also transport for the men who normally march. In many districts of the United Kingdom, the terrain is difficult and visibility limited, affording conditions which are admirably suited to the organization and tactics of German infantry. German infantry divisions landed at captured ports must be expected to have their full complement of supporting weapons. It is possible that infantry guns and mortars with their tractors will also be landed from small craft at beaches. Small parties of infantry landed as diversions will be unlikely to have many supporting weapons.

It is probable that the main functions of German motorized infantry and infantry landed as part of the main attack or attacks will be to follow up the advance of armoured divisions, mop up centres of resistance and occupy the territory overrun.

German infantry will be dependant on lines of communication for ammunition and stores, although limited supplies will probably be dropped by aircraft. As regards food, they will be likely to secure what supplies they can from the country; their effective action will depend greatly on interference with their lines of communication.

Engineers.

139. Engineer units will be among the first troops landed, whether the landings are effected in ports or on open beaches. In ports they may be employed for attacking fixed defences of all kinds and in removing demolition charges, etc. On open beaches their first tasks might be to clear beach mines and wire obstacles, using methods described in paragraph 132. For attacks on pill-boxes, flame throwers and special explosive charges would be used.

In the United Kingdom rivers and streams do not often present formidable obstacles, but engineers could be employed where necessary in ferrying and bridging operations with advanced armoured elements. In addition German engineer units, suitably mechanized, may be employed, as is usually the case in the German Army, in a combatant rôle, closely supporting A.F.Vs. and motorized infantry.

PART VI

Limiting Factors

Air Supremacy.

140. Probably the most important factor from the German point of view is the necessity to obtain sufficient air superiority to enable them to maintain effective fighter cover over the areas of their main landings. The restrictions involved have already been discussed in para. 109.

The enemy's fighter forces consist as far as is known at present of two types, the Me. 109 and the Me. 110. The bulk are Me. 109 short-range fighters, with an approximate endurance in the air of only one hour and twenty minutes. Whilst based overseas from this country they could be fully effective only in KENT and parts of SUSSEX, ESSEX and SUFFOLK. The Me. 110 has an approximate endurance in the air of two hours and thirty minutes, and could reach further afield to N.E. and S.W. England, but as far as is known the number of this type available does not exceed 400-500 machines.

Extra tanks can be carried by both types with consequent increase in range. Due, however, to the nature of the operation, *i.e.*, continuous and immediately effective fighter cover, it is not thought that these would be employed, as they adversely affect the performance of the aircraft, particularly in combat.

141. In view of these handicaps of the short range of the Me. 109 and the few numbers of the Me. 110, it is possible that the enemy might try to push his fighter bases forward by the capture of aerodromes in S.E. England or East Anglia and their subsequent use in connection with landings further afield (*see* also para. 109).

Such a procedure must necessarily be slow, owing to the time taken to transport and collect the necessary maintenance stores and install A.A. defence for the captured aerodromes. During this delay, which might be a matter of days, the bridgehead protecting the aerodromes would be open to ground attack and the aerodromes liable to bomber attack at short range.

142. From consideration of these air factors it would appear that, although initial landings are possible along the East and South coast of the British Isles, only those on the coasts of KENT, SUSSEX, ESSEX and SUFFOLK could be satisfactorily maintained and reinforced, others being restricted to what could be landed with them in the first instance.

This does not preclude the possibility of landings or feints elsewhere than in the S.E., as they would have a value in tying down reserves and dispersing our bomber effort on the beaches, but it does suggest that their effectiveness will last only as long as their initial supplies of petrol and ammunition.

General Vulnerability of Seaborne Attack.

*143. The main seaborne attack will be exposed to varying degrees of risk during the three stages of:—

(*a*) loading and embarkation;
(*b*) sea passage;
(*c*) disembarkation.

As regards the first stage, loading will require some seven to nine days, embarkation about 12 hours. Should the latter operation take place by night, the troops will, in a number of ports, need to stay on board during the succeeding day. On the other hand, embarkation by day will give an excellent opportunity to photographic reconnaissance aircraft of recording this sure indication of the start of invasion. The resultant warning would be available a few hours later.

Considerable interruption to the loading of equipment is therefore possible; little interference with or damage during the actual embarkation of troops can, however, be expected.

Forces which can be transported to any beach during the first night will probably be able to do little more than gain a footing ashore and only during the following days and nights can fully mobile formations be transported for exploitation. The disembarkation of troops, guns and vehicles on to open beaches by normal types of passenger and cargo vessels would be too hazardous in the face of naval and air opposition, and too slow. The main attack must, therefore, be restricted to T.L.Cs. and specially converted barges and, for that reason, confined to a short sea passage; the rate of disembarkation of such a force must be governed by the number of such craft available. The maintenance of an exploitation force, when it advances, by fresh formations with their supplies must be done by sea; the question of supply by air is discussed in para. 147.

Not the least of the enemy's difficulties would be those of a navigational and administrative nature imposed by a sea crossing with a large number of 6-knot barges. On the basis of the number of barges available, they would probably require to train about 5,000 coxswains and crews;

the barges would have to be capable of clearing their own harbours at the rate of about one per minute in the dark, without regard to confusion due to air attack and to casualties from mines. The craft would need to be fitted with wireless navigational aids, and coxswains would have to be able to use them effectively in spite of enemy night action. The earlier flights would have to keep station in the dark and in artificial fog with engines ill-adapted for the purpose. Perhaps the greatest navigational difficulty would be that of keeping slow and unmanœuvrable barges accurately on to the beach roadways in spite of cross-tidal streams, of smoke or heavy small arms fire and of wrecks of other barges.

Protection at Sea.

144. The vulnerability of the sea-borne forces on passage will depend upon the strength of the defender's forces encountered, the strength of the enemy's own escorts and the length of time in which the forces are in contact.

If the enemy is inferior in naval forces his only means of minimizing this vulnerability is to reduce the time during which he may be in contact with the defender's forces. This might be achieved by:—

(*a*) The use of long range shore guns, U boats, E boats (motor torpedo boats) and aircraft, assuring to the enemy temporary command of narrow waters; this restricts the area of probable landings to KENT and parts of SUSSEX and ESSEX.

(*b*) Concealment by night, fog or smoke, which might, however, re-act unfavourably on the enemy by creating confusion in his own forces.

(*c*) The dispersion of the landing forces over a wide area; this the enemy would probably do at least in the early stages in order to create diversions.

(*d*) The increase of the speed of the invasion craft; technically this is limited to about 6 knots for barges and 12 knots for merchant ships. Certain other craft including some tank landing craft might, however, attain much higher speeds (*c.f.*, paras. 43-53).

145. On the longer crossings it has yet to be proved that air escort can protect a convoy from attack by a superior surface fleet, and at present it appears unlikely

that it can do so at any considerable distance from its shore aerodromes. On the longer crossings, therefore, the alternatives open to the enemy are:—

(*a*) to draw off a large portion of the Home Fleet by stratagem;

(*b*) to confuse the issue by presenting the largest possible number of targets, some of which might be dummy convoys, consisting of ships in ballast.

Whilst some such system of strategem or confusion might achieve success for the initial landing, the problem of maintenance is entirely different. In that case the points to which the enemy is directing his convoys are fixed by his bridgeheads, and, therefore, are known. The only solution open to the enemy at that stage is one of force; he must be able to escort his convoys through our defence either on the sea or in the air, and the decisive factor must be the range and strength of the fighter forces required to escort the convoys and their bomber cover.

Supply Problems.

146. The success of the invasion must stand or fall on the ability of the Germans to maintain their forces after the initial landing supplies have been expended, and it is clear that their difficulties in this respect will be very considerable. While the enemy would not expect that all their assaulting forces could succeed in getting ashore, they would probably have to arrange for landing supplies and replacements at the rate of some 8-10,000 tons per day. The basis on which these figures are reached is shown in Appendix XXXIII. Forces based north and south of the Thames would require separate arrangements.

The proportions of these supplies which could be landed on to open beaches would depend on the number of special craft which had been provided, *e.g.*, craft designed to beach themselves, remain upright, and land supplies *via* special prows direct on to the shore (*vide* paras. 30-32). The continued supply of the invasion forces, as opposed to any improvised arrangements for the first few days, can only be carried out through properly equipped ports, in view of the high wastage rate of special craft and of other difficulties, including weather. It will be essential, therefore, for the Germans to secure, within or near the area of the main attack, ports capable of dealing with the volume of supplies envisaged. They will also need to organize without delay these ports as well as the supply echelons by road forward of them.

*147. The use of transport carrying aircraft which the enemy could spare from the transport of troops and divert to maintenance would be effective only for supplying isolated detachments of troops for a short period; it would not be possible to maintain or add materially to the maintenance of a force of any size, except possibly for a few days. The normal load of such aircraft would be about 1½ tons per sortie, subject, however, to the conditions of bulk involved. In any case, air transportation must be considered a diminishing asset.

148. The capacity of the ports in or near the probable area of the main attack (WASH to WEYMOUTH) is given in Appendix XXXIV, but allowance must be made for blocking and demolition operations by the defenders.

In EIRE the most useful port for disembarkation of troops and stores is CORK, but the GERMANS would probably attempt to capture and use other ports, (*see* Appendix XXXV).

A detailed study of the capacity of ports and beaches between NORTH FORELAND and DUNGENESS is given in Appendix XXXVI.

Lines of Communication.

149. In addition to the problem of landing supplies a secure line of communication is essential, and the only area in which the enemy appears to have any real hope of establishing this is the STRAITS OF DOVER area; by capturing the KENT coast and mounting guns or by capturing our guns and so having guns on both sides of the STRAITS, they might hope to deny them to our naval forces.

An attempt might be made to frustrate our air force by the maximum use of the hours of darkness. The enemy would make a determined effort to seize the vital area of the KENT coast, and to isolate it by airborne troops and possibly gas. This appears to be the only area in which they might establish adequate lines of communication.

PART VII

Choice of Time and Place

Time of Landing.

150. A dawn landing offers the possibility of surprise both as to the time and place owing to the concealment of the convoy by night movement. It has the added attractions of the protection given to a landing by a half light and early morning mist, together with a full day's light ahead in which to get a bridgehead well established and the necessary beach organization installed. Should, however, the enemy feel confident of establishing the necessary control of the sea by a combination of air and sea escort and long range guns, it is possible that he would be prepared to undertake the operation at any time of the day.

The period of two or three hours before high tide is usually considered the ideal time for a beach landing, owing to the advantages of landing men and stores closer inshore, and the reduced danger of assault craft fouling underwater obstruction or remaining aground when required for further tasks. These advantages largely disappear when the first flight ashore consists of A.F.Vs. impervious to small-arms fire whilst crossing the extended foreshore of a low tide, and it is, therefore, unsound to suppose that a landing must necessarily be confined to a dawn coincident with high tide.

The difficulties that may arise owing to the fact that high tide occurs at different times in different places are referred to in Appendix XXXVII.

Place of Landing.

151. The necessity for the capture of a suitable port for use in prolonged operations must affect the choice of beaches for initial landings. This choice does not mean that the beaches themselves need be close to the ports to be taken, since armoured formations could well advance up to forty miles in a day to attack the defences of a port in rear; beaches can, therefore, be chosen which have suitable positions inland on which to establish a bridgehead defence, and which offer a good line of approach from the beach to the port, unobstructed by any formidable obstacles easily defended against an enemy who will necessarily be short of bridging and other materials.

Sandy or shingle beaches with good gradients and exits and without strong cross currents are the most satisfactory; they are also the most obvious and, therefore, the most efficiently obstructed and guarded. It must be accepted, therefore, that the enemy in his constant efforts to achieve surprise may be prepared to attempt a landing at less suitable and more difficult sites, not excluding cliff-surrounded beaches with poor exits (*c.f.* para. 74).

Date of Attack.

152. There is every reason to believe that the enemy originally intended to attempt invasion in September, 1940, and he has no doubt made many detailed improvements and corrections to his plan since. There are, however, many factors, beside the completeness of the plan, that may influence the date for carrying it out, among which are commitments in other theatres, relative strength, and weather. Some factors which may influence the date in 1942 are referred to briefly in Appendix XXXVIII.

At all times a main requirement for invasion is a spell of fine weather sufficiently prolonged to cover the period required for sea-borne or intensive air operations.

Weather conditions likely to prevail in the south and east of England and their relation to combined operations are discussed at Appendix XXXIX.

Tidal Conditions.

153. Tidal conditions do not affect the question as to the general period in which invasion may take place; they are merely a guide as to the most likely time within each lunar period when invasion might be expected. They are much less important than the weather factor, and undue reliance should not be placed on them. Appendix XXXVII gives particulars of the coincidence of high water and dawn at various places on the South and East coasts (*see* also para. 150).

Warning of Attack.

*154. While no reliance can be placed on the receipt of warning of ***actual date or hour*** at which invasion is to be attempted, it is not possible for the invasion to be mounted without giving a number of indications of the final preparations. These indications would probably be obtained during the period of about three weeks prior to the earliest date at which the invasion could be launched; the fact that invasion is mounted does not, however, signify when it will be launched or that it will be launched at all. It would be possible for it to be kept mounted for a considerable period during which, subject to the fact that the assembled ships and craft in the ports would be exposed to air attack, it could start at any time.

A statement of the nature and the possible length of such warning is given in Appendix XL and a definition of R.N., R.A.F. and Army states of alert at Appendix XLI.

PART VIII

Concluding Remarks

155. These notes indicate the preparations which the enemy is known to have made to grapple with a problem in which there are three factors unfavourable to him:—

(*a*) The necessity of conveying the main bodies of his invading forces and subsequent supplies through waters in which he does not exercise naval control.
(*b*) The strength of our Air Force.
(*c*) The fact that he must fight a united country of high morale.

*156. It is clear on the other hand that the provision of shipping is not a limiting factor, except possibly in special invasion craft, especially T.L.Cs. and converted barges, and from the purely military aspect the enemy's resources are such that he would not be prevented from undertaking operations elsewhere simultaneously with those against the United Kingdom, either as a separate campaign or as a diversion to bring about a weakening of the defences of the U.K.; the limitations of his air resources, however, would make simultaneous major operations most difficult.

Apart from the military, naval and air factors which have been considered, political, economic and other factors must clearly play a large part in guiding the German High Command.

*157. There is very little doubt that invasion of the United Kingdom would be preceded by an attempt to sap the morale of the country; this would probably take the form of an effort to exploit the natural British tendency to complacency and indiscipline by prolonging to the last moment the sense of false security resulting from a period of inactivity against the United Kingdom; the next step might be to intensify the war of nerves by " terror " propaganda coupled with bogus peace feelers; heavy night bombing might be restricted until immediately before the launching of the invasion.

158. Finally, it cannot be too strongly emphasized that the Germans do not admit that there are any " rules " in warfare; any form of trickery or cunning, therefore, which would assist them in attaining their object must be expected.

It is also possible that they have, unknown to us, some gas of great potency or other secret weapon, although careful examination of all available evidence does not confirm the existence of such factors.

NOTES ON GERMAN PREPARATIONS FOR INVASION OF THE UNITED KINGDOM

APPENDICES

(For Table of Contents, *see* pp. 5–6)

APPENDIX III

GERMAN RAILWAY AND LONG-RANGE ARTILLERY

Serial No.	Calibre	Type	Length of Bore	M.V. f.s.	Weight of Shell	Maximum Range	Elevation	Traverse	Weight in Action	Remarks
			Cal.		lbs.	yds.	deg.	deg.	tons	
1	17 cm. (6·7 in.) ...	C.D. gun (may be on railway mounting).			140	26,000				A naval and coast defence gun of this calibre, as used in the last war, is believed to be in service. Figures quoted are those of 1918.
2	21 cm. (8·27 in.) ...	Gun, long range ...	160			81 miles				Unconfirmed. Particulars of this gun follow fairly closely those of the original Paris gun.
3	21 cm. (8·27 in.) ...	Railway gun ...				20,800		360		
4	22 cm. (8·66 in.) ...	Gun, long range (may be on railway mounting).		Probably not less than 4,000	235	At least 97,000 (55 miles)				Projectiles are of special rifled design with ballistic cap.
5	24 cm. (9·4 in.) ...	Railway gun ...	50	3,040	396	44,500	45	360	134	Life with full charge said to be 260 rounds.
6	28 cm. (11 in.) ...	Gun, long range (may be on railway mounting).				At least 105,000 (60 miles)				Projectiles are of special rifled design with ballistic cap, similar to those of No. 4.
7	28 cm. (11 in.) ...	Railway gun S.L.K. 65.	65	3,150?	720	45,000				Probably 11-in. naval gun put on railway mounting.
8	28 cm. (11 in.) ...	Gun, long range ...	125 to 130	5,900	660	125 miles	70			Unconfirmed. The figures quoted are, however, technically possible, but life would be very short.
9	30·5 cm. (12 in.) ...	C.D. gun (may be on railway mounting).				At least 44,000 (25 miles)				No details of the gun are known, but the projectile appears to be of naval origin.
10	38 cm. (15 in.) ...	C.D. gun		2,800		79,000 (45 miles)				Unconfirmed.
11	40·6 cm. (16 in.) ...	Railway gun ...	50	2,790	2,100	49,000	40	30		
12	42 cm. (16·5 in.) ...	Railway gun ...				25 miles				Unconfirmed.

APPENDIX IV

TABLE I

SHIPPING AT INVASION PORTS AS KNOWN AT JANUARY, 1942

(compiled from air reconnaissance reports)

	Battleships	Cruisers	Destroyers	Submarines	E. or R. Boats or M. T. Boats	Torpedo boats	Patrol vessels, Naval Auxiliaries and Minesweepers, etc.	Merchant vessels over 6,000 tons	Merchant vessels between 2,000 and 6,000 tons	Merchant vessels between 1,000 and 2,000 tons	Tankers	Barges	Other craft	Remarks
TRONDHEIM	...	...	...	1	...	1	8	3	3	11	...	2	2 catapult ships, 20 s.v.	
BERGEN	...	...	...	...	...	1	1	3	6	24	...	...	16 s.v.	
STAVANGER ...	...	...	...	...	...	...	4	3	3	3	1	...	20 s.v., 4 T-shaped rafts.	
KRISTIANSAND S.	...	...	...	...	...	...	6	1	8	9	3	...	1 depot ship, 8 s.v.	
OSLO	...	...	...	...	...	...	...	9	7	10	2	3	1 naval yacht, 32 s.v.	
AALBORG... ...	...	...	...	...	...	...	2	1	6	6	...	...	1 ferry, 6 s.v.	
COPENHAGEN ..	...	1	...	10	...	3	3	15	15	32	1	5	2 depot ships, 2 s.v., 10 coasters.	
STETTIN	...	...	1	4	...	4	5	13	17	12	...	300	1 a/c carrier, 11 T.L.Cs., 35 s.v., 8 coasters.	"Graf Zeppelin."
SWINEMUNDE .	...	...	1	...	2	3	5	4	1	4	1	47	43 T-shaped rafts, 1 minelayer, 1 T.L.C., 1 ferry, 13 s.v.	
KIEL	1	1	8	26	14	4	9	10	3	31	3	...	5 depot ships, 15 s.v. and coasters, 3 vehicle transports.	"Schleswig-Holstein", "Emden".
HAMBURG ...	...	...	1	12	...	...	1	14	16	39	3	400	17 s.v. and coasters.	

APPENDIX IV—*continued*

SHIPPING AT INVASION PORTS AS KNOWN AT JANUARY, 1942—*continued*

	Battleships	Cruisers	Destroyers	Submarines	E. or R. Boats or M. T. Boats	Torpedo boats	Patrol vessels, Naval Auxiliaries and Minesweepers, etc.	Merchant vessels over 6,000 tons	Merchant vessels between 2,000 and 6,000 tons	Merchant vessels between 1,000 and 2,000 tons	Tankers	Barges	Other craft	Remarks
CUXHAVEN	...	...	...	...	11	...	16	...	...	2	...	...	1 depot ship, 16 s.v.	
BREMERHAVEN .	...	...	1	2	1	...	1	3	2	4	1	20	1 minelayer, 14 s.v.	
BREMEN	...	1	4	5	...	...	1	...	16	15	...	60	2 coasters, 1 a/c ferry, s.v.	"Seydlitz."
WILHELMSHAVEN ...	...	...	1	4	3	3	...	5	...	...	2	20	19 s.v., some T-shaped rafts.	
EMDEN	...	...	...	1	...	...	...	4	5	9	...	120	3 flak ships, 14 s.v., s.c.	
DELFZIJL	...	...	...	...	...	...	...	...	...	2	...	208	2 s.v., s.c.	
GRONINGEN	...	...	...	...	...	...	...	...	...	...	...	220		
AMSTERDAM	...	...	...	...	6	...	...	6	...	8	...	500	15 s.v., 1 sloop, 2 ferries.	18 invasion barges.
DEN HELDER	...	...	...	1	...	...	3	...	...	...	...	8	13 s.v., s.c.	
IJMUIDEN	...	...	...	...	...	...	...	...	...	...	...	150	3 s.v.	
ROTTERDAM	...	1	1	1	8	2	...	9	15	16	...	472	16 s.v., 1 hospital ship, 1 sloop	
TERNEUZEN	...	...	...	...	...	...	...	...	...	...	...	50		
FLUSHING	...	...	...	...	1	...	5	...	...	1	...	8	2 ferries, 11 s.v.	
ANTWERP	...	1	...	...	...	...	1	2	6	2	1	750	15 Siebel ferries, 6 s.v.	"Hertog Hendrik", 290 invasion barges.

ZEEBRUGGE	...	...	...	...	...	...	...	...	...	...	...	15	4 Siebel ferries, 3 composite craft	
OSTEND	...	...	...	...	...	...	10	...	...	...	...	65	7 s.v.	
DUNKIRK	...	...	...	...	...	...	...	...	1	1	...	244	7 s.v.	
CALAIS	...	...	...	...	...	...	3	...	...	...	...	170		140 invasion barges.
BOULOGNE	...	...	...	...	...	...	...	...	...	2	...	70	2 s.v., 1 coaster, s.c.	56 invasion barges.
DIEPPE	...	...	...	...	...	...	1	...	...	...	...	48	9 s.v.	
LE HAVRE	...	...	...	...	1	3	1	2	2	2	2	123	1 Siebel ferry, 6 s.v., 7 coasters	60 invasion barges.
ROUEN	...	...	...	...	...	...	...	1	4	2	...	291	1 s.v.	
CAEN	...	...	...	...	...	...	...	...	1	1	...	12	s.c.	
CHERBOURG	...	...	...	...	...	...	4	...	...	2	...	9	3 Siebel ferries, 1 vehicle transport, 10 s.v.	
ST. MALO... ...	...	...	...	...	3	...	8	...	1	...	...	25	1 paddle steamer, 3 s.v.	
BREST	3	1	...	2	...	...	...	2	1	3	1	10	1 salvage v., s.v....	"Scharnhorst," "Gneisenau," "Gueydon," "Prinz Eugen."
LORIENT	...	1	...	5	...	...	5	...	...	4	...	6	1 depot ship, 5 s.v.	"Strasbourg II."
ST. NAZAIRE ...	...	...	...	2	...	2	9	2	...	...	5	12	17 s.v.	
NANTES	...	...	5	...	...	...	...	5	4	4	5	8	2 s.v.	
LA PALLICE	...	...	...	1	...	...	9	1	...	...	4	10	2 s.v.	
BORDEAUX	...	...	...	9	...	...	8	14	6	4	6	30	6 s.v.	

N.B.—(i) s.v.=small vessels, *i.e.*, under 1,000 tons.
s.c.=small craft, *i.e.*, harbour and fishing craft.

(ii) In addition to the barges shown in the above ports, considerable numbers of barges and other small craft may be in inland ports and waterways.

(iii) For description of German naval units referred to in Remarks column, *see* Appendix XVI.

APPENDIX IV—*continued*

TABLE 2

AVAILABLE INVASION CRAFT

Craft	No. believed available Dec., 1941	No. possibly available April, 1942	Remarks
T.L.Cs. ... . 9—11 knots Length, 150 ft. Draught, 4 ft. 4 in.	50—60 Max. 100	800 (under full scale effort)	Suitable for troops and A.F.Vs.
Barges (medium) ... ... s/p 250—700 tons 6—8 knots Draught, 4 ft. to 6 ft.	2,000 (50 per cent. converted)	3,000 (all converted)	Conversion of bows essential for disembarking vehicles.
Barges (small) ... ... s/p 120—200 tons 6—8 knots Length, 80 ft.	1,000	1,000 (60 per cent. converted)	
Dutch motor coasters ... 150—170 tons 9—10 knots Draught, 8 ft.	350	350	Suitable for supplies.
Siebel ferries ... ... Length, 80 ft. 7 knots (?)	250	250	Used either: (*a*) as flak platform and/or conveyance, or (*b*) as short-distance ferries for vehicles.
Train ferries ... ... 800—3,000 tons 10—16 knots	25	25	Suitable for troops and A.F.Vs.
Tugs, screw	1,700	1,700	Capable of towing two 300-ton barges at 6 knots.
Propulsion craft ... ... Length, 20 ft.	Unknown	Unknown	Alternative to tugs.
Assault craft ... ... (Fast motor boats, etc.) 20 knots or more	Numerous	Numerous	Larger craft might cross the Channel; smaller carried in M/Vs.

Note: "s/p" = self-propelled.

APPENDIX VI

MERCHANT VESSEL TONNAGE AND IDENTIFICATION

The following brief notes on tonnage and types of ships may be of assistance in the identification of M/Vs. which the enemy might use for invasion purposes, and in the interpretation of air photographs.

Tonnage Definitions.

1. When tonnage is used as a measure of identification, the kind of tonnage *must* be specified, *i.e.*:—

(*a*) gross tonnage (G.T.)
(*b*) deadweight capacity (D.W.C.)
(*c*) displacement.

Gross tonnage is in broad terms a measure of the size of a ship by internal cubic measurement (with certain limitations). Deadweight is a measure of the ship's cargo capacity. Displacement is used of naval units only.

It must be borne in mind that there is no regular relationship between G.T. and D.W.C., *e.g.*:—

Tanker 15,000 tons D.W.C. may be 7,000 tons G.T.

Passenger liner 4,000 tons D.W.C. may be 23,000 tons G.T.

M/V. Categories.

2. The following are the main categories into which M/Vs. fall, showing the terms of tonnage applied respectively:—

(*a*) Passenger liners, including cross-channel ships.	G.T.
(*b*) Cargo liners	D.W.C.
(*c*) Tramps	D.W.C.
(*d*) Tankers	D.W.C.
(*e*) Fruit ships	D.W.C. (or cubic ft. fruit capacity)
(*f*) Coasters	D.W.C.
(*g*) Trawlers	G.T.
(*h*) French fishing craft	According to type

M/V. Limits.

3. There is no direct relationship between G.T. and the length of a vessel, except in vessels of the same type. Table 1 overleaf shows the limits of length of the various types of M/V. above referred to, with their tonnage limits and speed limits.

Tonnage/Length Relationship.

4. The appended diagram (Table 2) shows a rough relationship between the gross and deadweight tonnages of M/Vs. and their length. It is emphasized that this applies to *cargo ships* only, and cannot be applied to passenger liners or craft of special design.

Likely Purposes.

5. The following types are likely to be used for the purposes described:—

Escort ships—
Fruit ships.
Cross-channel ships.
Trawlers.

"Flak" ships—
Fruit ships.
Trawlers.
Larger coasters, 500/1,200 tons G.T.

Naval auxiliaries—
Trawlers and drifters.

German Characteristics.

6. The main easily visible characteristics of German M/Vs. are:—

(*a*) Tall ventilator—derrick posts.
(*b*) Electric cranes on deck.
(*c*) Maierform bows (*i.e.*, curved and spoon-shaped as sailing yachts) and raking stems.
(*d*) Curved superstructures.

Speed.

7. The following factors may give useful indications of the speed and therefore potential danger of enemy M/Vs.:—

(*a*) *Outline.*

Fast ships built since 1935 may usually be identified by their curved streamlined superstructure.

(*b*) *Funnels.*

The height of funnels is a guide to age and therefore to some extent to speed. A tall funnel (*i.e.*, 30 ft. above the boat deck) indicates a ship of from 20 to 25 years, with a probable speed of not more than 10 knots. Coal-burning ships usually have a tall funnel, and few such ships of over 11 knots loaded speed have been built since 1914. The short funnels of modern motor ships are not more than 15 ft. high, are oval or pear-shaped in section and usually close to the navigating bridge; the speed of these vessels is usually between 13 and 17 knots.

(*c*) *Wake.*

Speed may be judged partly by wake, but it is to be noted that waves from any ship in motion spread from the bow at an angle of about 45°; a slow ship of broad beam pushes up the water immediately in front of her, and may give an impression of speed. A fast ship, while preserving 45°, makes cleaner water forward.

Wake aft is a fairly parallel track about half the width of the ship. A fast ship piles the water into fountain-like waves forward. The slow bluff ship pushes up water all round.

The usual division of ships into speed categories is as follows:—

Slow ships	7-11½ knots.
Fast ships	12-21 knots.
Very fast ships	21-40 knots.

APPENDIX VI—*continued*

TABLE I

SIZE OF MERCHANT SHIP TYPES

Type	Length Limits	Tonnage Limits	Speed Limits
	feet feet		
Passenger ...	400—750	13,000—40,000 Gross	15—24 knots
Cross Channel ...	300—400	3,000—7,000 Gross	17—24 knots
Cargo liner ...	350—440	9,000—12,000 D.W.C.	14—18½ knots loaded 15—21 knots light draft and by the stern.
Tramp	250—380	4,500—9,000 D.W.C.	8—11½ knots loaded 9½—12½ knots light
Tanker	360—550	8,000—15,500 D.W.C.	10—14½ knots loaded
	Machinery aft and no derricks except one on foremast.		
Fruit Ship ...	275—330	3,000—5,000 D.W.C.	15—19 knots
Coaster	100—280	100—250—1,500 D.W.C.	7—12½ knots
Trawler	80-150-220	80—1,000 Gross	Running free 8—14 knots
	Smallest trawlers are North Sea type.		
	Largest trawlers are French and Portuguese Grand Bankers.		
Drifter	80—95	70—100 Gross	9—10 knots

APPENDIX VI.

M/V (CARGO SHIPS) Table 2.

TONNAGE-LENGTH CURVES.

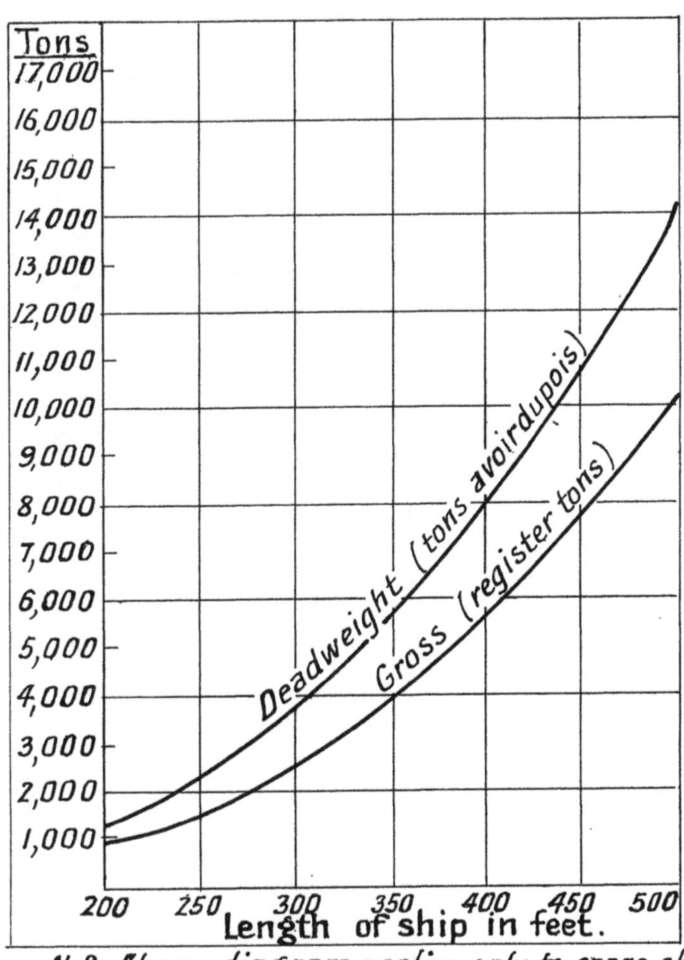

N.B. Above diagram applies only to cargo ships.

APPENDIX VIII

LOADING TABLE FOR M/Vs. AND BARGES

EQUIPMENT

Serial	Type of Equipment	Approximate dimensions in feet			Area occupied in sq. ft.	410-ton Barge loading		Ship loading number on deck only		Remarks
		Height	Width	Length		No. of rows	Number per barge	900 ton M.V.	4,200 ton M.V.	
	(a)	(b)	(c)	(d)	(e)	(f)	(g)	(h)	(j)	(k)
	A.F.Vs.—									
1	Amphibian F. IV H.E. 6·2 tons.	6·9	8·2	16·75	136·8	1	6	15	34	
2	Pz. Kw. I. 5·7 tons ...	5·6	8·0	12·5	100·0	1	7	15	34	
3	Pz. Kw. II. 9 tons ...	6·4	7·2	15·4	109·9	1	6	10	32	
4	Pz. Kw. III. 20–22 tons	7·75	9·75	17·6	172·25	1	6	6*	16*	*Hatch space NOT used.
5	Pz. Kw. IV. 22–24 tons	8·6	9·4	19·2	182·1	1	5	6*	8*	
6	Lt. armoured car Sd. Kfz. 222. 4·7 tons.	6 to 7·4	6·3	15·6	97·9	1	7	18	48	
7	Heavy armoured car (8 wheels).	9·0	8·0	17·5	140·0	1	6	10	24	
	M.T.—									
8	M./C.	3·3	2·6	7·2	18·7	5	72	...†	...†	†No limit for practical purposes.
9	M/C combination ...	3·3	4·5	8·5	38·3	2	24	45	168	
10	Limber/lt. lorry	7·5	7·2	21·3	153·4	1	4	....	22	
11	Hy., med. or sig. lorry ...	7·5	7·2	23·0	165·6	1	4	6	22	
12	Tractor	5·3	6·6	16·4	108·2	1	6	10	30	
13	Staff or W/T car	4·3	4·9	11·5	56·4	2	8	20	73	
14	Armd. comd. car	5·6	7·5	16·4	123·0	1	6	10	30	
15	Ambulance, 3 ton... ...	6·6	7·2	16·4	118·1	1	6	10	30	
	Guns—									
16	3·7-cm. (1·45-in.) A. Tk....	} 3·3	4·9	11·5	56·4	2	20	18	84	
17	7·5-cm. (2·95-in.) inf. ...	}								
18	15-cm. (5·9-in.) inf. ...	5·9	5·9	13·1	77·3	2	16	15	41	
19	10·5-cm. (4·14-in.) gun how.	5·3	5·9	20·0	118·0	2	10	8	22	
20	8·8-cm. (3·46-in.) A.A. ...	7·5	7·2	23·0	165·6	1	4	6	20	

APPENDIX IX

RE-ORGANIZATION OF GERMAN DIVISIONS

If the re-organization of normal armoured divisions to include only one tank regiment and certain modifications to motorized infantry divisions which have been brought into use in the Russian campaign are adopted for troops used in operations against the U.K., it is probable that the composition of the formations on which the figures given in para. 33 are based would be amended as follows:—

	Old assumed organization for invasion	New organization
Armd. Div.—		
Tanks, Hy.	12	...
Tanks, Med.	71	132
Tanks, Lt.	352	69
Total	424	201
M.C. Rifle Bns.	3	5
Fd. Arty. Btys.	2	3
Mot. Inf. Div.—		
Inf. Regts. (mot.)	3	2
M.C. Rifle Bn.	...	1

On this basis it is calculated that the aggregate effect on the numbers of barges required for transport would be as follows:—

Formation	Old organization	New organization
Armd. Div.	250	238
Mot. Inf. Div.	180	174

The following points must, however, be borne in mind:—

(*a*) Although no heavy tanks are at present included in the new organization of the armoured division, any which the enemy decided to use would no doubt be included in *ad hoc* formations.

(*b*) German army organization is very fluid and the adoption of any particular organization must be accepted with reserve; the composition of units is always likely, therefore, to be adapted to the special needs of a campaign.

APPENDIX X

NOTES ON CONVERTED BARGES AND T.L.Cs.

(*See* Fig. 1 overleaf)

Barges.

1. Low oblique photographs of BOULOGNE taken on 8th February, 1941, show for the first time the constructional alterations which have been carried out on the bows of barges. There appear to be two variations in treatment:

In type A the sides have been cut away, revealing a flat inclined surface leading from inside the hold down towards the waterline at the bows. The inclined plane is pointed and is not more than one foot above the waterline at the bow. The barge was trimmed by the stern at the time of photography, but trim is likely to be adjustable in this type of craft.

In type B the sides are cut away at approximately the same distance from the bows as in type A, but photographs show that the exit from the forward hold, instead of sloping gradually down towards the bow has a step in it, estimated at approximately one foot high. There appears to be no sound reason for having a step instead of a gradual incline and it would lessen the depth of the hold available for vehicles.

In addition to this difference between the two types, the decking in type B has not been removed on either side of the exit from the hold.

These barges were not down by the stern at the time of photography.

2. Although the position of the superstructure on the barges seems to vary considerably, in all cases it takes much the same form, *viz.*, a rectangular wall, possibly of concrete, approximately two feet thick and four feet high, open at the rear. Type A barges have two of these superstructures each. It is probable that these enclosures are for machine-gun crews whose task would be to cover the landing.

3. These barges may be of the self propelled type and have clearly been designed for the transport and rapid disembarkation of vehicles or troops, for either of which purposes they would appear to be suitable. In both types the actual bow is of normal shape, *i.e.*, slightly pointed, allowing the barge to retain its manœuvrability without undue detriment to the unloading of vehicles, and the forward hold is closed from the sea by a door. The superstructure would be suitable for mounting a machine-gun, and numerous experiments seem to have been carried out for the

Drawings and plans of this craft originally seen at the perspective drawing of type B; the machine-guns so mounted may include the 2-cm. (·79-in.) super-heavy M.G.

A number of wooden planks were seen on the quay of the WET BASIN at BOULOGNE where barges had previously been seen end-on to the quay with ramps. This, in conjunction with the photographs of the barges, suggests that these planks were separate and not fitted to the barges.

T.L.Cs.

4. Particulars of the craft referred to in para. 43 are as follows (*see* also drawing overleaf, Fig. 2):—

Length o.a.	154 ft. 2 in.
Depth to top of " hull "	14 ft. 2 in.
Draught (max.)	4 ft. 4 in. (app.)
Screws	3
Speed (assumed)	9-11 kts.
Beam	21 ft. 4 in.
Depth	8 ft. 3 in.
Tonnage (? displ.)	650
Power per screw available	(?) 200/300.

The dimensions make it clear that their A.F.V.-carrying capacity will be approximately equivalent to that of the 410-ton commercial barges referred to in Appendix VIII.

5. These craft have the following special features:—

(*a*) a double bottom, on which the A.F.Vs. rest, in place of the cement-filled floors of the barges. They have side tanks which presumably can be filled with buoyant material.

(*b*) a scow bow, excellent for beaching, with tongue-like ramp.

(*c*) a covered-in and possibly armoured fore and aft hull.

(*d*) underwater propulsion by aero engines which are reported to be three Benz " V " type. The use of aero engines is logical in the programme reported, which requires 2,400 units of about 150 h.p. output, and, allowing for replacements, might embarrass normal i.c. engine output for other work.

(*e*) square lines, which permit of easy fabrication and welding.

Three of these craft have been seen under way in ROTTERDAM harbour; they appear perfectly handy, even in a narrow and tide-swept harbour; they make little wash, are fairly silent, and must be considered as eminently practical craft.

APPENDIX XI

NOTES ON SIEBEL FERRIES

(*See* paras. 47 and 48 and drawings overleaf)

1. Description of these craft is as follows:—

Length... ...	Approximately 80 ft. } Other dimensions as in drawings overleaf.
Breadth ...	46 to 50 ft.
Speed	About 7 knots, perhaps up to 12 knots.
Propulsion ...	Propulsion is by two engines, one in each of the aftmost compartments, each driving one screw; in some cases large outboard motors may be used, and in others it is believed that propulsion is supplemented by air screws in the stern of the craft in case the water propellers foul the beaches.
Construction ...	Two steel hulls (probably "Herbert" sectional pontoons) joined together by a platform reported to be of wood; distance between the hulls is about 28 ft.; cross members connecting the two hulls are approxi mately 1 ft. 6 ins. apart and strengthened by lattice bracing. A centrally placed "turret" measures about 15 ft. by 20 ft. The front of the craft is straight, *i.e.*, the fore end is squared off and there is no evidence of bow-shaped construction. Their shallow draught reduces the vulnerability of these vessels to minefields.

Drawings and plans of this craft, originally seen at ANTWERP and copied from air photographs, are at Fig. 1, overleaf.

The "Herbert" pontoon itself can be dismantled into eight separate parts, each of the six central units being about 6 ft. 6 in. long, and each of the two end units about 9 ft. 10 in. The Siebel ferry itself is, therefore, capable of being transported by rail without difficulty; this form of construction also provides some safeguard against sinking if the craft is holed.

2. Fig. 2, is a drawing compiled from a photograph and description of a craft seen at CONSTANZA.

Comparison with the drawings of the vessel at Fig. 1, shows clearly that the CONSTANZA vessel is a variation of that craft, and confirms to some extent the multi-purpose nature of the craft, being used in this case as a true ferry. The main constructional details and dimensions agree in almost every respect with those of the Siebel ferries, the use to which the deck is put being the only important difference. The use of anchor davits, which is common German river-practice, suggests that this variation of the Siebel ferry may be primarily intended for work in rivers and estuaries where fast currents are likely to be encountered.

Although Siebel ferries are known to have been used also for Flak purposes in the CONSTANZA area, the description and drawings make no reference to this aspect.

It is believed that most of the craft used as ferries have a light deckhouse amidships, and that some of this type also carry at least one 8·8-cm. Flak gun.

3. The sketch and drawings at Figs. 3 and 4 are based on a Siebel ferry which in October, 1941, formed part of the defences of SOLA aerodrome, Norway. This craft, whose construction agrees with that described in para. 1, is reported to be propelled by an aeroplane engine in each after compartment driving under-water propellers; both engines together give the vessel a speed of 6-7 knots. This vessel was brought from Germany in sections, with the engines already fitted, and was assembled in Norway. There are no cabins apart from that seen in the centre of the craft, and no hatchways to the compartments other than the engine hatch seen to the right of the sketch.

The armament of this vessel is:—

Three 8·8-cm. A.A. guns.

Two 2-cm. A.A. M.Gs.

One 4-m. base stereoscopic range-finder with predictor.

All weapons were permanently fixed to the deck and platforms respectively. Ammunition was stored in loose cases on the deck.

The craft was normally moored to the side of the fjord, and on an alarm being given was warped out some distance from the shore; firing commenced, however, while the vessel was being moved out, and without waiting to reach the final position.

The number of the crew was given as eighty-six (which appears high), but there were no living quarters on board, the men being billeted ashore. There is only sufficient room on the vessel for a few small vehicles, and long narrow ramps apparently suitable for embarking and disembarking vehicles were carried.

APPENDIX XIII

PARTICULARS OF TYPICAL GERMAN AND SCANDINAVIAN FERRIES

German Train Ferries

Vessel	Length	Beam	Gross tonnage	Speed when loaded	Draught
	feet	feet			ft. inch
Schwerin	334	59·1	3,133	13½ k.	?
Mecklenburg	282	46	1,547	13 k.	?
Preussen	355·8	51	2,954	16½ k.	16 0
Deutschland	356·1	51	2,972	16½ k.	16 0

Note.—The "Preussen" and the "Deutschland" are designed for stern loading.

Danish Train Ferries (owned by Danish State Railways)

Vessel	Length	Beam	Gross tonnage	Speed when loaded	Draught
	feet	feet			ft. inch
Svea	222·9	34·5	800	10 k.	?
Dan	222·9	34·5	800	10½ k.	?
Orehoved	222·9	34·5	800	10½ k.	?
Helsingborg	177·0	32·1	530	10 k.	?
Danmark	133·2	51·5	2,730	15½ k.	14 0
Prins Christian ...	293·6	44·9	1,900	13¾ k.	?
Christian IX	290	48·6	1,590	15⅛ k.	?
Odin	290	48·5	1,580	15⅛ k.	14 6
Fenris	180	36·0	760	12½ k.	13 1
Freia	240·4	40·9	1,430	15¼ k.	?
Korsor	315·8	56·6	2,365	15 k.	13 1
Nyborg	336·3	56·6	2,255	15 k.	13 6
Sjaelland	336·3	56·6	2,595	15 k.	13 2
Storebaelt	346·8	56·6	2,942	16½ k.	13 1
Morso	132·1	27·9	284	10 k.	9 2

Danish and Norwegian Car Ferries

The following particulars are available of Danish and Norwegian car ferries which would be used by the Germans for transport of A.F.V. or M.T.

Vessel	Length	Beam	Gross tonnage	Speed when loaded	Draught
	feet	feet			ft. inch
Heimdal	246·1	38·6	980	13 k. (side and end loading)	11 6
Kronborg	145·5	36·8	480	10¾ k. (end loading)	9 6
Isefjord	185·9	35·3	622	13	?
Djursland	154·2	33·0	361	13	8 5
Skagerak I	222·5	38·2	1,281	18	13 0
Peter Wessel	223·2	42·9	1,415	16	14 5

APPENDIX XIV

DESCRIPTION OF MILITARY ASSAULT BOATS

These are standard army engineer equipment and consist of light, wooden, keelless boats designed for speed and capable of taking 16 men with full equipment in addition to the crew of 2. The boat is driven by an outboard " motor oar " which is a completely separate unit and takes the form of a protected propellor at the end of a 6-ft. enclosed shaft driven by a 12 h.p. 4-cylinder air-cooled engine. The boat is claimed to do a maximum speed of 15 knots in still water fully loaded, but it is considered unlikely that a speed of more than 9 knots can, in fact be attained. The boat and outboard motor are taken down to the water's edge separately, 8 men being required for the boat and 6 for the motor oar.

APPENDIX XV

GERMAN E BOATS AND R BOATS

(*vide* also Para. 60)

(*a*) The following is a brief description of E boats:—

Performance.—Length 105 ft. 6 in.; beam 16 ft.; maximum speed 34·5 knots; draught 5 ft.-6 ft.; minimum speed 9 knots; endurance at 22 knots 600/800 miles; at 12 knots 1,300 miles. Tonnage 60/70 tons. The crew numbers 23. There is another type of E boat slightly smaller and less powerful.

Defensive Armament.—1 20-mm. free cannon mounted amidships with no protection for the gunner but an arc of fire of 180° in all directions. Three machine guns carried unmounted in the wheelhouse. Depth charges could possibly be used to embarrass low-flying aircraft attacking from astern.

Armour.—The wheelhouse is said to be bullet-proof, but is probably not. Fuel tanks, either just forward or aft of the engine, are self-sealing. The engine is probably armoured with 6/7-mm. (about ·25-in.) plate. A great deal of intricate and sensitive mechanism is exposed and easily susceptible to damage by gunfire. The hull and decks are probably all steel.

Defensive Tactics.—For evasion E boats rely on smoke screens, high speed, fire power and extreme manœuvrability. A close arrowhead formation can concentrate accurate fire from 400 ft. downwards. An E boat can turn through 90° in 8/10 seconds and its powers of acceleration are even more noteworthy. Owing to the noise prevalent on board, an aircraft has a good chance of approaching altogether unheard, though E boats have of course no " blind spot ".

Offensive Tactics.—E boats mostly fire their torpedoes unselectively from 800/1,100 yards when convoys are sighted, then make off at full throttle. It does not appear that torpedo tubes can be reloaded at sea. Ruses to distract the attention of victims by dazzling them, by laying mock smoke screens, and by dressing up as a sailing ship, are not uncommon.

Co-operation with Aircraft.—There is not yet any evidence of direct R/T communication between aircraft and E boats engaged on operations. Messages from at least one reconnaissance unit are passed by land-line between the aircraft's ground station and the principal E boat base at IJMUIDEN. Aircraft also co-operate in an attack by the dropping of flares and light signals.

(*b*) The following are the principal differences between E boats and R boats, which are often confused:—

	E boat	R boat
Function	Attacks on shipping by torpedo, grenade, cannon gunfire and depth charges. 50 per cent. faster than R boat.	Minesweeping, minelaying, sea rescue, anti-submarine patrol. No torpedoes carried.
Identification ...	Work mostly by night and are not camouflaged, but painted a grey-white colour. Wake at speed visible ½ a mile behind boat.	Work mostly by day and are camouflaged. R boat minesweeping leaves three-track wake. Appears much smaller than E boat, though it is of 50 per cent. greater tonnage.
Areas of Operation	NORTH SEA as far as the HUMBER, particularly off NORFOLK Coast (YARMOUTH to SHERINGHAM. ENGLISH CHANNEL as far as PLYMOUTH.	Close to Continental coast.
Formations ...	Usually in tight "vic".	Usually in line abreast.

Particulars of only two classes of R boat are known, and are as follows:—

Type	Length	Displacement (Normal)	Speed	Armament	Engines
R. 1–16	85 ft. 6 in.	45 tons	18 knots	One 0·79-in. A.A.	Two 600 h.p. M.A.N. Diesel twin screw.
R. 17–40	106 ft.	90 tons	18 knots	Two 0·79-in. A.A.	Two 900 h-p. M.A.N. Diesel twin screw.

APPENDIX XVI

GERMAN FLEET AS ESTIMATED AT 31.12.41

15-inch Battleship	TIRPITZ	
11-inch Battle Cruisers	GNEISENAU SCHARNHORST	
11-inch Pocket Battleships	ADMIRAL SCHEER LÜTZOW	
Old Battleships ...	SCHLESWIG-HOLSTEIN SCHLESIEN	
Aircraft Carrier ...	GRAF ZEPPELIN	Completing.
8-inch Cruisers ...	HIPPER PRINZ EUGEN SEYDLITZ ...	Trials not yet commenced.
6-inch Cruisers ...	NURNBERG LEIPZIG KÖLN EMDEN	
Destroyers	18	
T.Bs.	34	
M.T.Bs.	80 (Approx.)	
Auxiliary Craft ...	600–700	

APPENDIX XVII

OPERATIONAL STRENGTH OF G.A.F.

1. *Estimation of Available Forces.*

(*a*) The following table shows the estimated total German Air Force strength on 1st April, 1942. Thus, if every aircraft is pressed into service the total of all types available would be about 13,000 on the basis of 80 per cent. serviceability:

—	1st Line I.E.	R.T.Us.	Reserves	Training	Total	80 per cent. serviceability	Sorties, 1st day
Long Range Bombers	1,450	380	720	680	3,230	2,580	1,700
Bomber Reconnaissance... ...	460	40	250	110	860	690	450
Dive Bombers	340	60	160	200	760	610	900
S.E. Fighters	1,020	120	500	340	1,980	1,590	2,000
T.E. Fighters	410	40	200	110	760	610	470
Army Co-op.	430	30	230	100	790	630	480
Coastal	200	30	140	60	430	340	200
	4,310	700*	2,200	1,600*	8,810	7,050	6,200
Transport	950	...	100	450	1,500	1,200	
						8,250	

* *Note.*—It is estimated that two-thirds of the R.T.U. organization is now devoted to advanced training and that only one-third is available as a fully trained reserve. Thus, for operational considerations, the strength of R.T.Us. should be reckoned as 230 and that available from training as 1,600 + 470 = 2,070.

In addition there are some 5,000 elementary training types.

The figures given for the number of sorties on the first day represent the maximum effort. This effort would rapidly decline and would probably be reduced to about 50 per cent. by the third day.

(*b*) *Gliders.*—The number is uncertain. It is thought that the G.A.F. may possess about 2,400, mainly 10-seater operational type with a few other larger types, but that by April, 1942, the numbers available may, if required, have been increased to some 5,000, of which about 4,000 would be of the small type.

(*c*) *Parachutists.*—There are sufficient trained parachutists for the aircraft available; the limiting factor is one of carrying capacity and not of trained personnel.

(*d*) *Airborne troops.*—These need not have special training. The numbers and equipment that can be carried are also limited by aircraft available.

2. *The Rôle of the Aircraft.*

The use to which the aircraft can be put is generally speaking self-evident, but the following are available for special duties:—

Minelayers—

Total	600	long range bomber types.
80 per cent. availability.	480	
Total	100	coastal types.
80 per cent. availability.	80	

The majority of these are probably capable of carrying torpedoes if required. These are included in the totals given in paragraph 1 above.

All bomber reconnaissance aircraft are potential heavy bombers and it is thought that about half the available force could be diverted for this purpose.

3. *Transport Aircraft.*

It is thought that the number of Ju. 52 aircraft available is about 1,500, of which approximately 1,200 would be airworthy at the commencement of operations. It is certain that a number of these would be required for urgent transport duties during an invasion attempt. (In the battle of Crete it was estimated that out of a total of 650 some 100 to 150 were so employed.) It is estimated that between 300 and 400 would be required for this purpose during operations against this country. It is probable, therefore, that some 800 to 900 Ju. 52s. would be available for an airborne invasion. If the few other suitable transport types are included, the maximum force is estimated at 1,000 aircraft.

4. *Losses.*

The losses during the first few days of an operation must be conjectural, but, as a tentative estimate, it is thought that transport aircraft might be reduced by the third day to 40 per cent. of the initial total and operational aircraft to 50 per cent.

APPENDIX XVIII

PRINCIPAL G.A.F. TYPES OF OPERATIONAL AND TRANSPORT AIRCRAFT WITH RADII OF ACTION

(*See* also accompanying map Appendix XIX).

Description	Type	Radius of action in Miles		Normal load
		Normal condition	Extra tanks	
				lbs.
L.R. bombers and bomber recce. ...	Do. 17	350	...	2,200
	Do. 217	U.K.	...	4,400
	He. 111	U.K.	...	2,200
	Ju. 88	U.K.	...	3,000
Heavy bombers ...	Fw. 200	U.K.	...	4,400
Dive bombers ...	Ju. 87	117	350	2,000
T.E. Fighters ...	Me. 110	340*	650*	...
S.E. Fighters ...	Me. 109 } Me. 109F }	150*	360*	...
Troop Transport ...	Ju. 52	350	415	10-12 men
	Ju. 90	U.K.	...	10 tons
Sea-planes	He. 115	550	...	3,000 lbs.
	Do. 18 (flying boat)	800	...	nil. for max. range

* Figure includes no combat allowance.

APPENDIX XX

ORGANIZATION, EQUIPMENT AND TRANSPORT OF AIRBORNE FORMATIONS

Composition of Parachute and Gliderborne Formations

1. 7 Air Division contains three parachute rifle regiments (1, 2 and 3) and divisional troops which include:—

Parachute Arty. Bty.: 7·5-cm. (2·95-in.) mtn. guns.
Parachute A.Tk. Bn.: 3·7-cm. (1·45-in.) or 2-cm. (0·79-in.) A.Tk. guns.
Parachute M.G. Bn.

Each parachute rifle regiment is organized very much like an ordinary infantry regiment; it has slightly fewer heavy M.Gs. and heavy mortars, but more L.M.Gs. and machine carbines; it contains the usual 13 and 14 Coys. (inf. gun and A.Tk.).

Among the corps troops of XI Air Corps are:—

Parachute A.A.M.G. Bn. (2-cm. A.A.M.Gs.).
Parachute Engineer Bn.
Parachute Medical Unit.

Units of these are normally attached to the parachute rifle regiments for operations.

1 Assault Regiment is organized in much the same way, though the composition of its 13 and 14 Coys. is unknown, and its equipment varies (as befits shock troops for special operations). Units seem designed to operate independently. There is a possibility that this regiment will be expanded to a division.

Equipment.

2. (*a*) Parachute troops take, besides all the standard weapons of the infantry battalion, the following:—

2-cm. (0·79-in.) A.A.M.G.
3·7-cm. (1·45-in.) A.Tk. gun.
2-cm. (0·79-in.) A.Tk. gun model 41.
7·5-cm. (2·95-in.) inf. gun.
7·5-cm. (2·95-in.) mtn. gun.
10-cm. (3·94-in.) mortar, smoke.
Small flamethrower (probably).
12-cm. (4·72-in). mortar (probably).
Motor cycles.
A.Tk. mines and explosives.

(*b*) Gliderborne troops are known to take all weapons of the infantry battalion, including the 8·1-cm. mortar. It is not known whether they take anything heavier.

(*c*) Airlanding troops have taken beside the above, the following equipment in small quantities:—

5-cm. (1·97-in.) A.Tk. gun.
15-cm. (5·9-in.) infantry gun.
"Tracked motor cycle" for haulage.

It is not confirmed that any A.F.V. has so far been transported by air in operations.

Aircraft Required to Transport Units and Formations.

3. The numbers of aircraft required to transport the undermentioned units *at one lift* are as follows:—

Parachute division: 4 Transport Groups	880 aircraft.
Parachute rifle regiment: 1 Transport Group.	220 aircraft.
Assault regiment: 1 Transport Group with gliders.	220 aircraft and gliders.
Parachute rifle battalion: 1 Transport Wing.	53 aircraft.
Parachute company (rifle or heavy): 1 Transport Squadron.	12 aircraft.
Airlanding division	900-1,000 aircraft.

It should be noted that the transport of a whole division *at one lift* is at present purely theoretical.

APPENDIX XXI

ORGANIZATION OF AN AIR-LANDING INFANTRY DIVISION

(as used in operations in HOLLAND, May, 1940)

Divisional H.Q.—

One M.C.D.R. sec.
One M.P. det.

H.Q., mot. A.A. M.G. bn.—

Four mot. A.A. M.G. coys.

H.Q., Div. Sigs.—

One W/T coy.
One tel. sec.

H.Q., Div. Recce. unit—

Two cyclist sqns.
One cavalry gun troop.
One pioneer troop.

H.Q., Div. A.Tk. bn.—

Two A.Tk. coys.

H.Q., Div. Engineer bn.—

One engineer coy.

H.Q., Inf. regt.—

One sig. sec.
One recce. pl.
Three bns. each of three rifle coys. and one M.G. coy.
One inf. gun coy.
One A.Tk. coy.
One lt. inf. column (without vehicles).

Inf. regt. organized as above.

H.Q., Div. arty. regt.—

One sig. sec.
Three btys. (two btys. of three tps., one of two).

One coy. and one pl. div. medical unit.

Three pls. div. supply coy. (without vehicles).

Strength (*approximate*)

270 officers.
7,130 other ranks.
Total 7,400 all ranks.

Armament (*approximate*)

5,000 carbines.
400 machine-carbines.
110 A.Tk. rifles.
60 5-cm. (2-in.) light mortars.
36 8·1-cm. (3·16-in.) heavy mortars.
8 7·5-cm. (2·95-in.) infantry guns.
2 7·5-cm. (2·95-in.) cavalry guns.
30 2-cm. (0·79-in.) A.A. and A.Tk. M.Gs.
200 L.M.Gs.
60 H.M.Gs.
30 3·7-cm. (1·45-in.) A.Tk. guns.
32 7·5-cm. (2·95-in.) mountain guns.

APPENDIX XXII

TECHNICAL DETAILS OF GLIDERS

Operational Gliders.

1. Three types of operational gliders are known to be in use by the German Air Force:—

(i) D.F.S. 230. Wing span approximately 71 ft. 6 ins.

(ii) Gotha 242. Wing span approximately 79 ft.

(iii) Large gliders with a wing span of approximately 180 ft. ("Merseburg" type).

D.F.S. 230. (Drawings appended at Fig. 1.)

2. The D.F.S. 230 is a high wing monoplane glider with a wing span of approximately 71 ft. 6 ins. The crew consists of one pilot and nine passengers or troops with full equipment. The seats are fitted on a boom placed along the fuselage, the pilot being placed in the nose of the fuselage.

The total flying weight of this type of glider is between 4,200 lbs. and 4,600 lbs., depending upon the make-up of the load. The typical load for a unit of ten men is 2,450 lbs., which includes six rifles and one heavy machine gun.

The following tables 1 and 2 give typical estimated ranges of the D.F.S. 230 glider towed by a Ju. 52 tug. Table 3 has been extracted from a German document, and shows a few typical cases of free gliding ranges of the D.F.S. 230 after release. (Fuller extracts from this document are given in Table 4 of this Appendix).

TABLE 1. Range of towing aircraft

Tug: Ju. 52, three B.M.W.-132 H engines developing a maximum power of 830 h.p. each at 3,600 feet; tug loaded to a normal flying weight of 22,000 lb., including 530 gallons of fuel (normal maximum tankage) and about 1 ton of load.

No. of gliders towed	1	3
Cruising speed at 5,000 ft. m.p.h.	100	100
Still air range ... ... miles	850	550
Take off distance (over 50 ft. screen) ... ... yds.	600	1,000

TABLE 2. Range of towing aircraft

Tug: as above, but overloaded to 25,000 lb., including 1,000 gallons of fuel (with supplementary tanks in fuselage) and no disposable pay load.

No. of gliders towed		1	3
Cruising speed at 5,000 ft.	m.p.h.	100	100
Still air range	miles	1,600	1,100
Take off distance (over 50 ft. screen)	yds.	800	1,400

Note.—The ranges in Tables 1 and 2 are estimated for ideal conditions in still air. No allowance is made for evasive tactics, navigational errors, head winds, etc. It is assumed that the glider is towed for the whole range, *i.e.*, the tug does not return to its base.

TABLE 3. Range of gliders

—	Head wind		Following wind	
Wind speed	9 m.p.h.	37 m.p.h.	9 m.p.h.	37 m.p.h.
Gliding distance after release from 6,600 ft. (in miles)	20	11·5	25	33
Gliding distance after release from 13,000 ft. (in miles)	42	24	52	69

From aerodynamic considerations alone the maximum possible speed is not likely to exceed 185 m.p.h. at 4,000 ft. when one glider is towed by a Ju. 52, or 165 m.p.h. at 4,000 feet for a train of three gliders. It is extremely unlikely that these speeds will be realized in practice, as a limitation may be imposed by the strength and stiffness of the glider structure. This limitation may be of the order of 130 m.p.h.

It is of interest to compare these estimates with information obtained from a P/W, pilot of a D.F.S. 230 glider, captured in Crete: a typical operational altitude is given as 5,000-6,000 ft. and the cruising speed (one Ju. 52 towing one glider) 105 m.p.h. The full load optimum gliding speed (after release) is 70 m.p.h. and the landing speed in still air 35-40 m.p.h.

The various lengths of towing cable are 200, 260, 325 and 400 feet. The 200 ft. length is the shortest and for use on small aerodromes. Generally speaking it is preferable to have a longer cable in order to control the behaviour of the glider in flight.

The glider is normally fitted with an undercarriage which is jettisoned on operational flights, but whatever the method of take-off special runways are not essential.

Flaps are fitted to the wings to steepen the gliding angle. Both the tug and the glider are provided with release hooks, the release hook of the tug being used only in an emergency.

The flying instruments consist of a rate of climb indicator, two altimeters (coarse and fine reading), turn and bank indicator, air speed indicator and compass. The electric installation includes a headlamp and three recognition lights, the necessary current being supplied from a 24-volt accumulator. Thus, although the glider is not fully equipped for blind flying, it might be used at night, provided the tug carries the necessary navigational equipment. Operational training on gliders at night is a prominent feature of the glider training programme.

It is possible that luminous paint may be used on the towing cables for night flying.

Gliders probably of the D.F.S. 230 type were used in the capture of Fort Eben-Emael in Belgium in May, 1940, and also in the capture of Crete in May, 1941, though not in any considerable numbers.

Gotha 242. (Drawings appended.)

3. The specifications of this glider are as follows:—

Designation:	Gotha Go. 242.
Duty:	Troop and freight transport.
Crew:	2 (pilots).
Airframe characteristics:	Twin boom monoplane. Detachable nacelle of tubular metal construction. Wings, tail booms and tail unit of wooden construction. Dual control. Skid and wheel undercarriage, the wheels being jettisonable. Rear end of nacelle, hinged at trailing-edge of wing, lifts upwards making an opening 7 ft. × 6 ft. for loading.
Dimensions:	Span: 79 ft. Length: 52 ft.
Armament:	8 gun positions for 8 light guns with belt feed. Type of gun not specified.
Useful loading and freight capacity:	The useful load is 5,300 lbs. or 21 fully equipped troops (in addition to the pilots).

Normal towing a/c.:	One Ju. 52.
Freight stowage space:	20 ft. × 8 ft. × 6 ft. 6 ins.
Armour:	1st pilot's seat fully armoured, thickness 8 mm.
Maximum towing speed:	149 m.p.h.
Maximum gliding speed:	180 m.p.h.

175-180 *ft. Span Gliders (" Merseburg " type).*

4. The existence of these gliders is confirmed both from reports and aerial photographs. This may be the type reported to have a seating capacity of 40-50 men, but precise details cannot yet be given.

A rough estimate shows that two Ju. 52 tugs would be necessary. Loaded as in Table 1 and towing one of these gliders carrying 40 men, the take-off would be about 800 to 1,000 yds. over a 50 ft. screen. The corresponding still air range would be of the order of 700 to 800 miles.

An interesting point is that this type of glider may have a tricycle under-carriage and the front part or nose of the fuselage may be detachable.

The over-all width of the fuselage is about 9 ft., and although the type of construction is not known, it would be reasonable to assess the internal width at about 8 ft. As the fuselage is either rectangular or oval it is possible to assume that the available height of the freight compartment will be more than 8 ft.

Taking the most optimistic estimate the useful load is not likely to be more than 10 tons, but in view of the size of the fuselage the troop-carrying capacity could not exceed 40 to 50 fully-equipped men.

260-275 *ft. Span Glider (possibly known as the GOLIATH).*

5. Reports have been received of a very large glider having a wing span of approximately 260-275 ft. The latest information is that this is of the twin fuselage type with accommodation for 140 troops plus equipment. The passengers are said to be carried in two cabins, but up to the moment no further details are available.

This new glider is considerably larger than the Merseburg type (175-180 ft. wing span) already referred to, but it is not thought that these reports can be dismissed as improbable. The useful load of 16 tons obtained from another source seems a possible figure, and tallies with the figure of 140 men given above. It is not considered that the technical difficulties involved in building so large a glider are insurmountable.

Take-off.

6. There is no reliable information on this subject; it is possible, though unlikely, that rockets may be used to reduce take-off distance.

Use may be made of the " winch " method, consisting of a powerful engine driving a heavy flywheel. The glider is towed rapidly by a cable which is wound on a drum geared to the flywheel and released when air borne.

This method is readily adaptable for use with the training type of glider.

Glider Tugs.

7. A detailed study is being made of the various types of German aircraft which could be used as tugs. The following aircraft have been mentioned in this connection; in general the Ju. 52 appears to be the most suitable type.

Ju. 52	Ju. 86
He. 46	Me. 109
He. 45	Me. 110
He. 126	W. 34
He. 123	

The towing of gliders by bombers such as the He. 111, Ju. 88 and Do. 17 is, of course, a technical possibility. It is very unlikely, however, that a Ju. 88 or He. 111 can take off with a glider in tow whilst carrying its full external bomb load, consisting of two or four large or medium calibre bombs. These machines would have to operate with a very reduced bomb load, internally stowed, and the eventual ranges would not be greatly in excess of those obtained with a Ju. 52. From the purely technical point of view, therefore, there appears to be no advantage in employing modern bombers as glider tugs.

In addition to the above, it has been found that the equipment of the G.A.F. includes an aircraft known as the B 71 and described as a tug.

The B 71 is the Russian SB bomber of 66 ft. span, having a normal weight of 17,400 lb. It is fitted with M. 100 engines of 860 h.p. at 13,000 ft. The B 71 is also used as a twin-engined trainer, but its primary duty is towing. Taking into account the size and power plant of this aircraft, it is reasonable to assume that it will be used mainly as a glider tug.

It is not known how many of this type of aircraft the G.A.F. possesses, but the number is not thought to be large.

A proposal has appeared in the German press of a method proposed by Horten Bros. for a tug of a special design. These designers have for some considerable time been working on tail-less aircraft, and it is a possibility that special glider tugs have been designed on this principle for sporting glider requirements.

Gliders-Trains.

8. An article in the U.S.A. publication "Flying" shows a Russian twin-engined aircraft towing eleven gliders in "V" formation (five in each arm of the V and the eleventh at the rear in the centre). No details are given as to the size of these gliders or of the method of take-off, but from information available no difficulty should be experienced in taking off with a number of gliders. The limiting factor is the power available for take-off and climb.

Small gliders are more likely to be used singly with small aircraft than a large number of small gliders towed by one tug.

Night Flying.

9. It has been shown that night flying in clear weather is a practical possibility.

Tank and Freight-carrying Gliders.

10. The general situation with regard to glider-borne tanks, based on recent information, is referred to in para. 79; from the technical point of view it is possible to design a glider tank which on loading would shed its wings, tail, etc., and go into action as an ordinary tank. It is thought, however, that specially re-designed tanks would have to be used, as the pick-up points for the airframe would otherwise prove a difficult problem; the shape of an ordinary tank also leaves a great deal to be desired from the aerodynamic point of view.

Twin-boom aircraft recently seen at ELEUSIS (Greece) have been identified as the Gotha 242 (*see* para. 3); similar aircraft were photographed near DERNA (Libya), in flight, towed by Ju. 52 aircraft and specimens were found there later, abandoned by the enemy.

The possibility of this being a special form of glider cannot be disregarded. Freight or even a tank could be "suspended" under the centre section of the wing, thus overcoming the various difficulties in connexion with the fitting of a tail and nose piece to the tank itself. However, the span mentioned above would correspond to a useful load of probably just over one ton, which does not seem to correspond to any known type of small tank. In the case of transport of special freight which may be difficult to stow into an ordinary 72 ft. glider, a twin boom design would probably solve the problem. In the case of transport of special supplies, *e.g.*, petrol, bulky aircraft, spares, aero-engines, etc., detachable containers could be designed.

Further investigations are being made to classify smaller types, *i.e.*, less than 60 ft. span. It is thought, however, that these smaller gliders would not be standard troop or freight carriers, as the G.A.F. seem to standardize on the 72 ft. type which is being found in a great number of air photographs. The smaller types are probably trainers and advanced trainers for pilots and troops, together with a small number of possibly non-standard transport gliders.

TABLE 4

EXTRACT FROM GERMAN GLIDER RANGE TABLES

Wind-speed	Height of release	Direct Head Wind		Wind at Right Angles		Direct Tail Wind	
		Ground Speed	Horizontal Range	Ground Speed	Horizontal Range	Ground Speed	Horizontal Range
m.p.h.	feet	m.p.h.	miles	m.p.h.	miles	m.p.h.	miles
9·3	3,300	67·12	8·75	75·82	9·65	85·76	11·18
	6,600	71·47	19·7	80·17	22·0	90·11	25·0
	9,900	75·82	30·8	84·52	34·20	94·46	38·80
	13,200	80·17	42·0	88·87	46·55	98·81	52·50
	16,500	85·76	53·0	94·46	58·75	104·41	66·20
18·6	3,300	57·8	7·45	74·58	9·60	95·09	12·43
	6,600		16·78		21·75		27·96
	9,900		24·80		33·80		43·50
	13,200		35·0		45·99		59·04
	16,500		44·5		57·80		74·58
27·9	3,300	48·47	6·2	71·47	9·0	104·41	13·35
	6,600		13·67		20·51		30·45
	9,900		21·4		32·00		47·23
	13,200		28·85		43·10		64·01
	16,500		36·66		54·69		80·79
37·3	3,300	39·15	4·97	66·50	8·70	113·73	14·55
	6,600		11·50		19·55		32·94
	9,900		17·70		30·45		50·96
	13,200		23·85		41·30		69·30
	16,500		30·45		52·20		87·32

REMARKS

1. The Tables are valid for the following conditions: Flying weight 2,000 Kg., jettisoned undercarriage, no objects to be suspended in the air flow.

2. The longest range is obtained from all altitudes with the air speed indicator at 71·4 m.p.h. (gliding angle in still air 1 : 20).

3. 660 ft. have been deducted for landing manœuvres.

4. The wind speeds in the tables are average mean speeds between the released height and earth.

APPENDIX XXIII

BRIEF PARTICULARS OF POSSIBLE GERMAN AIRBORNE TANKS

T.K.—

Weight—2·5 tons.
Length—8 feet 6 inches.
Armament—1 7·9-mm. or 1 20-mm. A.Tk.
Armour—10-mm.
Speed (max.)—28 m.p.h.
Crew—2.

S.I.—

Weight—3·5 tons.
Length—8 feet 6 inches.
Armament—1 37-mm. and 1 M.G.
Armour—14-mm.
Speed (max.)—28 m.p.h.
Crew—2.

Pz. Kw. I.—

Weight—5·7 tons.
Length—12 feet 6 inches.
Armament—2 34 M.Gs.
Armour—18-mm. (front), 14-mm. (side).
Speed (max.)—32 m.p.h.
Crew—2.

Pz. Kw. II.—

Weight—9 tons.
Length—15 ft. 4 inches.
Armament—1 20-mm., H.M.G., 1 L.M.G.
Armour—20+20-mm. (front), 15-mm. (top), 18-mm. (sides).
Speed (max.)—25 m.p.h.
Crew—3.

APPENDIX XXIV

USE OF LARGE-SCALE SMOKE CLOUD

Behaviour of the Smoke Cloud.

1. Invasion of the U.K. requires a wind blowing off the Continent towards the British Isles. During the summer months such a wind will consist of warm air which, on passing over the colder water, will give rise to favourable conditions for the travel of smoke. Not only will the rate of upward diffusion of the smoke be small, but any tendency for the cloud to rise as a whole during day-time will also be reduced. These favourable conditions will still prevail at night and the tendency for the cloud to "lift" will then be completely absent. The bodily "lifting" of a cloud is essentially a day-time phenomenon and only occurs to a marked degree with dark coloured smokes. It occurs with white smoke only under exceptional conditions which would be unsuitable for the present purpose.

Vertical Visibility.

2. During the first 10 miles of travel the height of the smoke cloud would not exceed about 2,000 feet, and the opacity of the smoke would be great. Such a cloud would undoubtedly be most effective against aerial observation. Even if aircraft descended into the smoke cloud, the zone of vision would be restricted to a small circle immediately beneath.

At greater distances from the line of emission the same effect would prevail. It would then be necessary for the aircraft to descend further through the smoke before becoming able to detect vessels on the water, and the zone of vision would again be severely restricted to the vertical.

At a distance of 50 miles from the line of emission the average visibility within the cloud would probably be less than 1,000 yards, making flying in the cloud a matter of considerable hazard.

Horizontal Visibility.

3. At a distance of 10 miles from the line of emission the horizontal visibility at sea level within the cloud would not exceed a few hundred yards. At greater distances down wind the visibility would improve only very slowly, and even at distances of the order of 50-100 miles the visibility would probably still be less than a mile.

It has to be realized that it is one of the chief characteristics of a large smoke cloud that, after the initial stages, the conditions within the cloud remain sensibly constant over a long distance of travel. In this respect such a cloud differs fundamentally from a cloud produced from a single or "point" source. Unless this principle is borne in mind, an erroneous view is liable to be taken of the probable visibility within a cloud after long distances of travel.

The estimated visibility of about a mile might exercise an important effect upon naval operations.

Rate of Emission.

4. On the assumption that a white smoke (*e.g.*, chlorsulphonic acid) were used it is believed that under average meteorological conditions a rate of emission of 20 tons per hour per mile of front will produce a screen which is effective against aerial observation by day for a distance down wind equal to about 5 times the length of the line of emission. Thus the use of 60 tons per hour on a 3 miles front would be effective for a distance of about 15 miles and the area screened would be about 15 by 3=45 square miles. There can be little reasonable doubt that this rule can be applied at least approximately to a smoke cloud emitted on a front of about 20 miles length.

Meteorological Conditions.

5. (*a*) The meteorological conditions necessary for the travel of a smoke cloud would be:—

(i) Wind blowing from the required direction.

(ii) Wind speeds not less than 5 miles per hour and probably not more than 15 miles per hour, since any higher wind would cause a rough sea, and the projected landing would be on a lee shore.

(o) AVERAGE number of days in the years 1929-1938 on which winds of stated strength occurred within given limits of direction:—

Area from which smoke screen might be emitted	Limits of wind direction	Area of English Coast on which smoke screen might arrive	Month	Number of days		Total
				Force 2	Forces 3 & 4	
1. Southern North Sea.	E.-S.E.	LOWESTOFT to the SOUTH FORELAND	Jan.	0·3	2·1	2·4
			Feb.	0·6	2·1	2·7
			March	0·5	3·2	3·7
			April	1·0	1·8	2·8
			May	2·6	2·4	5·0
			June	2·5	1·7	4·2
			July	2·2	2·8	5·0
			Aug.	1·1	3·9	5·0
			Sept.	2·0	2·0	4·0
			Oct.	1·4	1·5	2·9
			Nov.	1·0	4·1	5·1
			Dec.	0·1	1·0	1·1
2. Straits of Dover	E.-S.W.	SOUTH FORELAND to BEACHY HEAD	Jan.	2·5	7·1	9·6
			Feb.	1·5	3·7	5·2
			March	2·7	6·7	9·4
			April	2·9	4·2	7·1
			May	5·3	5·5	10·8
			June	5·9	4·3	10·2
			July	7·1	10·8	17·9
			Aug.	2·6	8·4	11·0
			Sept.	4·7	6·5	11·2
			Oct.	2·8	6·2	9·0
			Nov.	3·4	7·4	10·8
			Dec.	1·1	6·4	7·5
3. English Channel	S.E.-S.W.	BEACHY HEAD to START POINT	Jan.	1·4	6·4	7·8
			Feb.	0·8	3·2	4·0
			March	1·0	6·0	7·0
			April	2·3	4·0	6·3
			May	3·3	5·7	9·0
			June	3·8	4·3	8·1
			July	6·8	8·8	15·6
			Aug.	2·2	5·6	7·8
			Sept.	3·9	5·3	9·2
			Oct.	2·6	5·5	8·1
			Nov.	2·4	6·2	8·6
			Dec.	0·4	5·2	5·6

Notes.—Force 2=4-7 m.p.h., Forces 3 and 4=8-18 m.p.h.

(*c*) MAXIMUM number of days in the years 1929-1938 on which winds of stated strength occurred within given limits of direction:—

Area from which smoke screen might be emitted	Limits of wind direction	Area of English Coast on which smoke screen might arrive	Month	Number of days		Total
				Force 2	Forces 3 & 4	
1. Southern North Sea.	E.-S.E.	LOWESTOFT to the SOUTH FORELAND	Jan.	1	8	9
			Feb.	4	5	8
			March	2	7	7
			April	2	3	4
			May	6	6	11
			June	7	5	12
			July	5	6	10
			Aug.	3	8	9
			Sept.	5	6	8
			Oct.	3	4	7
			Nov.	2	9	11
			Dec.	1	3	3
2. Straits of Dover	E.-S.W.	SOUTH FORELAND to BEACHY HEAD	Jan.	5	15	20
			Feb.	5	7	9
			March	5	10	14
			April	6	9	12
			May	8	9	14
			June	11	13	22
			July	11	20	28
			Aug.	12	14	24
			Sept.	7	11	16
			Oct.	8	10	13
			Nov.	6	14	16
			Dec.	5	14	14
3. English Channel	S.E.-S.W.	BEACHY HEAD to START POINT	Jan.	4	15	19
			Feb.	3	10	11
			March	3	11	14
			April	6	6	10
			May	6	10	14
			June	8	15	19
			July	12	13	25
			Aug.	7	11	18
			Sept.	7	8	14
			Oct.	8	10	14
			Nov.	6	10	12
			Dec.	2	12	12

Notes.—(i) Force 2=4-7 m.p.h., Forces 3 and 4=8-18 m.p.h.

(ii) The figures in columns 5 and 6 of the above table may refer to different years, and do not necessarily, therefore, give the total shown in column 7.

Special Diurnal Conditions.

6. The conditions set out in paragraph 5, covering a period of ten years, have been deduced from the surface pressure gradients at 0700 G.M.T. and 1800 G.M.T.; they

do not, therefore, take into account local effects such as land and sea breezes and the consequent bearing which the time of day might have upon the possible frequency of emission of gas or smoke across the Channel.

It must be borne in mind that land and sea breezes and similar local effects may be regarded as modifications of the general wind system prevailing at any given period; they are contributions to or components of these general wind systems. The following notes give a general indication of the two main modifications likely to arise:—

(*a*) *Land and Sea Breezes.*—In June, July and August land and sea breezes are generally well developed, but are less so in May and September. The sea breeze effect will generally introduce an on-shore contribution between about 1000 and 2000 G.M.T. at well-exposed places on the South and East coasts, on seven or eight days in each of the months June to August, and on about four or five days in May and September. On the other hand an off-shore wind, the land breeze, may be apparent on two or three days in June, July and August, and on one or two days in other months, and will be felt principally from about two hours before dawn to two hours after dawn. It may be taken that the land breeze would be force two, whereas the sea breeze would reinforce an on-shore wind, under favourable conditions, to the extent of 10 m.p.h. or more; *i.e.*, a wind of force three might be increased to about force five, and a wind of force two to force four. It must, however, be remembered that the land and sea breeze effects are very much dependent on the topography of the coast line and the above can therefore only be accepted as a general indication.

(*b*) *Inversion of Temperature.*—The other diurnal effect which should be taken into consideration is the following: in a spell of quiet weather during summer with a light wind from the Continent to the British Isles, temperatures are likely to be high over the Continent. After the air leaves the coast of the Continent the lowest layers of the air will be cooled by the coolness of the sea surface, with the result that an inversion of temperature will occur over the sea. In consequence gas released from the Continent would tend to be held near the surface as the convection over the land which would have diffused the gas would be counteracted when the air passed over the sea. The most likely time for these conditions would be the late afternoon or evening. This condition would last during the night and it might continue over the sea during the day (unless the gas were dense enough to absorb an appreciable amount of solar radiation, which seems unlikely). Although, as mentioned, late afternoon or evening would be the most likely time for the enemy to take advantage of this effect, which would, of course, be favourable for the emission of gas, the time of arrival in England of gas so discharged would depend upon the speed of the wind and the distance to be traversed.

7. *Wind Forces.*

The approximate equivalents in m.p.h. of wind forces are as follows:—

Wind force	Speed in m.p.h.	Description
0	Less than 1	Calm.
1	1—3	Light Air.
2	4—7	Light Breeze.
3	8—12	Gentle Breeze.
4	13—18	Moderate Breeze.
5	19—24	Fresh Breeze.

APPENDIX XXV

1. COAST CATEGORIES OR U.K. AND N. IRELAND

Area	Mileage suitable for landing			Mileage not suitable for landing	Total mileage of coast line
	A.F.Vs.	Other arms	Total		
EAST COAST OF SCOTLAND	52	20	72	381	453
BERWICK—WASH (middle)	137	41	178	150	328
WASH (middle)—PORTSMOUTH (excl.) ...	178	98	276	137	413
PORTSMOUTH (incl.)—LANDS END ...	118	28	146	282	428
NORTHERN IRELAND	1	98	99	111	210

Beaches Suitable for T.L.Cs. and Barges.

2. As stated in Appendix X, the maximum draught of the T.L.Cs. referred to is approximately 4 ft. 4 in., and they will normally ground in 4 ft. of water at a point 40 ft. abaft the hinged ramp; the draught of barges converted for A.F.V.-carrying is also about 4 ft.

For Pz. Kw. I, which has a water-fording capacity of 2 ft., a depth of water of 2 ft. or less must be found at the end of the ramp; this condition will only obtain on beaches of a gradient of 1 in 20 or steeper.

Below is a table showing the water-fording capacity of the four commonest types of German tank and an estimate of the minimum gradient of beaches on which they could be landed from the T.L.C. or barge:—

Type of tank	Water fording performance	Required beach-gradient
Pz. Kw. I (5·7 tons)	2 feet	1 in 20.
Pz. Kw. II (9 tons)	2 feet 6 inches	1 in 27.
Pz. Kw. III (18—20 tons) ...	2 feet 11 inches	1 in 40.
Pz. Kw. IV (22 tons)	3 feet 6 inches	1 in 80.

Similar considerations apply, of course, to the landing of M.T. vehicles. The normal fording capacity of German M.T. will be considerably less than that of A.F.Vs. (probably approximately 1 ft. 6 in., requiring, therefore, a slope of 1 in 20 or steeper), but modifications either to the vehicles themselves or to the landing craft might enable them to be landed in beach conditions more nearly approximating those for A.F.Vs. referred to above.

In the table at Appendix XXVI particulars are given of the gradients of beaches between THE WASH and WEYMOUTH which are suitable for the landing of tanks; it is emphasized that these particulars refer only to the actual disembarkation of tanks and may include beaches which natural or artificial features ashore might render unsuitable for A.F.V. landing.

APPENDIX XXVI

BEACH GRADIENTS BETWEEN THE WASH AND WEYMOUTH

(*See* para. 110 and Appendix XXV)

IMPORTANT.—These figures are from coastguards' reports, and attention is particularly drawn to the fact that, owing to the effects of wind and weather and to other causes, some of the gradients given in this table may be incorrect; formations and units should, however, be able to check any particular gradient by measuring the distance between high and low water on the same day and ascertaining through the Naval Liaison Officer the "range" of tide for *that particular day*.

It is also emphasized that the particulars given in this table relate to the suitability of beaches for the disembarkation of vehicles and may, therefore, include beaches which, owing to natural or artificial features *ashore*, are unsuitable for this purpose.

N.B.—In the following table the undermentioned abbreviations are used :—

H.W. = High water mark (mean). H.W.S. = High water mark (spring tides).
L.W. = Low water mark.
B.L.W. = Below low water mark. B.H.W. = Below high water mark.
A.L.W. = Above low water mark. A.H.W. = Above high water mark.

Serial No.	Area	County	Mileage	Gradient	Remarks
1	HUNSTANTON to BLAKENEY POINT.	Norfolk	20	Varying from 1 in 10 to 1 in 15.	
2	to WEYBOURNE (incl.) ...	"	5	Steep slope	Less steep west of CLEY towards BLAKENEY POINT.
3	to SHERINGHAM (incl.) ...	"	4	Steep at all states of tide.	
4	to BACTON (incl.)	"	14	Flat A.H.W. 4-ft. ridge at H.W. Shelves to 1 in 10.	

Appendix XXVI—*continued*

Beach Gradients Between The Wash ard Weymouth—*continued*

Serial No.	Area	County	Mileage	Gradient	Remarks
5	HAPPISBURGH	Norfolk	4	Flat A.H.W. 1 in 10 B.H.W.	
6	to HORSEY GAP	"	7½	Flat A.H.W. 1 in 40 B.H.W.	
7	to CAISTER	"	8½	Flat A.H.W. Varying from 1 in 15 to 1 in 10 B.H.W.	Spring tides very high.
8	to GORLESTON	"	5	Flat A.H.W. 1 in 40 B.H.W. becoming 1 in 20 at GORLESTON.	
9	to CORTON	Suffolk	4	Varying from 1 in 40 to 1 in 20.	
10	to KESSINGLAND	"	10	Varying from 1 in 40 to 1 in 20.	
11	to SOUTHWOLD	"	7	1 in 40.	Spring tides very high.
12	to MINSMERE	"	6	Varying from 1 in 40 to 1 in 10.	Steepest point is between DUNWICH and MINSMERE.
13	MINSMERE to THORPENESS	"	4	1 in 5 to L.W., 1 in 20 B.L.W.	
14	to 1 mile S. of ALDEBURGH	"	3½	1 in 5 H.W. to L.W., 1 in 25 B.L.W.	Small shoals inshore changing frequently.
15	to entrance to R. ORE ...	"	10	1 in 7 H.W.S. to H.W., 1 in 7 to L.W.	
16	to BAWDSEY POINT ...	"	5	1 in 4 from H.W. to L.W., 1 in 20 B.L.W.	
17	BAWDSEY FERRY to FELIXSTOWE DOCK	"	7	1 in 12 from H.W. to L.W., 1 in 20 B.L.W.	Gradients on all beaches liable to be affected by wind changes. Steepest usually between H.W.S. and H.W. (Nos. 13–28)
18	HARWICH to NAZE ...	Essex	6	1 in 30 from H.W. to L.W., 1 in 40 B.L.W.	
19	to HOLLAND SLUICE ...	"	7	1 in 30 from H.W. to L.W., 1 in 50 B.L.W.	
20	HOLLAND HAVEN to CLACTON PIER	"	3½	1 in 12 from H.W. to L.W., 1 in 15 B.L.W.	
21	to COLNE POINT	"	7	1 in 20, thence 1 in 30.	
22	MERSEA ISLAND	"	5	1 in 40, thence 1 in 50.	
23	OSEA ISLAND to BRADWELL QUAY	"	4	1 in 30, shallowing B.L.W., then steeper.	
24	BRADWELL to ST. PETER'S POINT	"	3	1 in 30, steeper B.L.W.	
25	to HOLLIWELL POINT ...	"	8	1 in 50 to L.W., thence steeper.	Mud flats.
26	to BURNHAM-ON-CROUCH	"	5	1 in 20 from H.W. to L.W., thence steeper	
27	FOULNESS ISLAND to SHOEBURYNESS POINT	"	15	1 in 40 for 3 miles in depth, thence steeper	
28	to CANVEY ISLAND ...	"	10	1 in 30 from H.W. to L.W., thence steeper	

29	WARDEN POINT to SHELLNESS (Isle of SHEPPEY)	Kent	3½	1 in 12 at H.W., 1 in 200 at L.W.
30	GRAVENEY to HAMPTON	,,	4	6 in 100 at H.W., 1 in 500 at L.W.
31	to HERNE BAY PIER ...	,,	1¼	10 in 175 at H.W., 1 in 150 at L.W.
32	RECULVER TOWERS to MINNIS BAY	,,	3	10 in 175 at H.W., 1 in 150 at L.W.
33	MINNIS BAY	,,	½	1 in 56.
34	to MARGATE HARBOUR	,,	1½	1 in 48.
35	to FORENESS	,,	1½	1 in 44.
36	BOTANY BAY	,,	1/10	1 in 60.
37	KINGSGATE BAY	,,	2/5	1 in 80.
38	JOSS BAY	,,	2/5	1 in 80.
39	STONE BAY	,,	4/5	1 in 80.
40	BROADSTAIRS BAY ...	,,	¼	1 in 40.
41	DUMPTON GAP	,,	¼	1 in 80.
42	RAMSGATE SANDS ...	,,	1	1 in 34.
43	PEGWELL BAY	,,	3	1 in 45.
44	R. STOUR to KINGSDOWN	,,	12	1 in 5 at H.W., 1 in 9 at L.W.
45	ADMIRALTY PIER, DOVER, to SHAKESPEARE CLIFF TUNNEL, E. entrance.	,,	1½	1 in 10 at H.W., 1 in 40 at L.W.
46	SHAKESPEARE CLIFF TUNNEL, W. entrance, to ABBOTS CLIFF TUNNEL, E. entrance.	,,	1	1 in 30 at H.W., 1 in 60 A.L.W., 1 in 120 B.L.W.
47	ABBOTTS CLIFF TUNNEL, W. entrance, to WARREN HALT.	,,	1¼	1 in 70 at H.W., 1 in 20 B.H.W., 1 in 100 at L.W.
48	to COPT POINT	,,	1	1 in 10 at H.W., 1 in 25 B.H.W., 1 in 120 at L.W.
49	FOLKESTONE RY. PIER to VICTORIA PIER.	,,	½	1 in 7 at H.W., 1 in 20 B.H.W., 1 in 50 at L.W.
50	to SEABROOK	,,	2½	1 in 8 at H.W., 1 in 120 at L.W.
51	to HYTHE	,,	2¾	1 in 10 at H.W., 1 in 100 at L.W.
52	to GRAND REDOUBT ...	,,	2½	1 in 10 at H.W., 1 in 100 at L.W.
53	to DYMCHURCH	,,	2½	1 in 12 at H.W., 1 in 100 at L.W.
54	to ST. MARY'S BAY ...	,,	1½	Varying from 1 in 4 to 1 in 12 at H.W., 1 in 30 at L.W.

APPENDIX XXVI—*continued*

BEACH GRADIENTS BETWEEN THE WASH AND WEYMOUTH—*continued*

Serial No.	Area	County	Mileage	Gradient	Remarks
55	to LITTLESTONE	Kent	1¾	1 in 20 at H.W., 1 in 55 at L.W.	
56	to GREATSTONE	,,	1	Varying from 1 in 13 to 1 in 6 at H.W., 1 in 55 at L.W.	
57	to LYDD	,,	2	1 in 5 at H.W., 1 in 77 at L.W.	
58	DUNGENESS POINT ...	,,	2½	1 in 2 at H.W., 1 in 10 at L.W.	
59	DUNGENESS W. to DENGEMARSH	,,	2½	1 in 8 uniform.	
60	to GALLOWAYS	,,	3	Varying from 1 in 6 to 1 in 12.	
61	to E. end of CAMBER ...	Sussex	1	1 in 8 at H.W., 1 in 40 at L.W.	
62	to RYE HARBOUR ...	,,	2¼	1 in 13 at H.W., 1 in 40 at L.W.	
63	to RYE LIFE BOAT HOUSE	,,	¾	Varying from 1 in 30 to 1 in 15.	
64	to CLIFF END	,,	5	1 in 12 at H.W., 1 in 48 A.L.W., 1 in 87 B.L.W.	
65	E. GROYNE, HASTINGS, to WARREN SQUARE	,,	1	1 in 5 at H.W., 1 in 10 B.H.W., 1 in 40 at L.W.	
66	to ST. LEONARD'S PIER ...	,,	1	1 in 20 at H.W., 1 in 40 at L.W.	
67	to GALLEY HILL ...	,,	2½	1 in 13 at H.W., 1 in 30 at L.W.	Rocks extending seaward about 800 yds. E. of GALLEY HILL.
68	to 1 mile W. of BEXHILL	,,	2	1 in 20 at H.W., 1 in 40 A.L.W., flat at L.W.	
69	to COODEN	,,	1¼	Varying from 1 in 15 to 1 in 20 at H.W., 1 in 120 at L.W.	
70	to PEVENSEY SLUICE (NORMAN'S BAY)	,,	1½	Varying from 1 in 10 to 1 in 20 at H.W., 1 in 120 at L.W.	
71	to HOLYWELL (EASTBOURNE)	,,	5½	1 in 7 A.H.W., 1 in 12 H.W. to L.W.	Seawall for 2 miles E. of HOLYWELL.
72	BIRLING GAP	,,	⅛	1 in 30 uniform.	Gap leading from beach obstructed.
73	CUCKMERE RIVER ESTUARY	,,	½	1 in 10 from H.W. to half-flood, 1 in 30 from thence to L.W.	Marshes behind beach.
74	SEAFORD HEAD to NEWHAVEN (E. PIER)	,,	2½	1 in 7 uniform.	High level railway parallel to shore, then marshes.

75	NEWHAVEN BREAKWATER to BURROW HEAD	„	¾	1 in 7.	
76	KEMPTOWN (BRIGHTON) to SHOREHAM HARBOUR	„	5	1 in 7 A.H.W., 1 in 10 B.H.W.	
77	to ½-mile Westward	„	½	1 in 7 A.H.W., flat B.H.W.	
78	to ANGMERING-ON-SEA ...	„	8	1 in 7 A.H.W., flat B.H.W.	
79	to LITTLEHAMPTON ...	„	2¾	1 in 30 at H.W., 1 in 80 at L.W.	
80	to ALDWICK	„	6¼	1 in 30 at H.W., 1 in 80 at L.W.	
81	to PAGHAM BEACH ...	„	1¼	1 in 20 at H.W., flat at L.W.	
82	to PAGHAM HARBOUR ...	„	¾	1 in 15 at H.W., flat at L.W.	
83	to SELSEY LIFEBOAT SLIP	„	2	1 in 9.	
84	to WEST WITTERING ...	„	7	Flat.	
85	HAYLING ISLAND (SANDY POINT to GUNNEN POINT)	Hants	3¼	1 in 5 A.H.W., 1 in 10 H.W. to L.W.	
	ISLE OF WIGHT				
86	WHITECLIFF BAY ...	„	½	1 in 56 at L.W.	Water comes to within a few feet of cliff foot at H.W.
87	SANDOWN BAY	„	5	1 in 75 at L.W.	
88	BONCHURCH	„	¼	Varying from 1 in 37 to 1 in 50 at L.W.	Rocky formations on beaches.
89	VENTNOR	„	⅖	1 in 35 at L.W.	
90	ST. CATHERINE POINT to BROOK POINT	„	4	1 in 45.	Sand and shingle with ledges of rock.
91	to COMPTON BAY ...	„	5	1 in 50.	
92	FRESHWATER BAY ...	„	⅛	1 in 20.	
93	GOSPORT to SOUTHAMPTON	„	14½	1 in 20.	Shelving B.L.W. is fairly steep to steep.
94	to HURST CASTLE and KEYHAVEN	„	22	Varying from 1 in 20 to 1 in 40.	
95	to HIGHCLIFFE	„	5	Varying from 1 in 20 to 1 in 40.	
96	to BOURNEMOUTH ...	„	8	Varying from 1 in 30 to 1 in 40.	
97	to POOLE	„	3¼	Varying from 1 in 40 to 1 in 25.	
98	to SWANAGE	Dorset	3	1 in 25.	
99	SWANAGE (to PEVERIL POINT)	„	2	1 in 30.	

APPENDIX XXVI—*continued*

BEACH GRADIENTS BETWEEN THE WASH AND WEYMOUTH—*continued*

Serial No.	Area	County	Mileage	Gradient	Remarks
100	to DURLSTON HEAD ...	Dorset	1	1 in 30.	Shelving B.L.W. is fairly steep to steep. Rock formations and ledges scattered over the bays.
101	ST. ALBAN'S HEAD ...	„	1¼	1 in 20.	
102	to KIMMERIDGE BAY ...	„	¾	1 in 40.	
103	to WARBARROW BAY ...	„	¾	1 in 30.	Shelving B.L.W. is fairly steep to steep.
104	to LULWORTH COVE ...	„	½	1 in 30.	
105	to ST. OSWALD'S BAY ...	„	1½	1 in 30.	
106	RINGSTEAD	„	¾	1 in 20.*	
107	OSMINGTON	„	⅓	1 in 30.*	
108	SHORTLAKE...	„	1	1 in 15.*	
109	BOWLEAZE COVE ...	„	¼	1 in 25.	* Indicates that after southerly or south-easterly gales, temporary ridges of shingle are formed, which would then be very much steeper than the gradient indicated.
110	PRESTON to GREENHILL	„	1½	Varying from 1 in 3 to 1 in 10.*	
111	to WEYMOUTH PIER ...	„	¾	1 in 50.	

APPENDIX XXVII

TIME ON PASSAGE FROM INVASION PORTS

From	To approx. nearest point of England	Approx. distance direct in nautical miles	Length of passage in hours: 6 knots, Barges	10 knots, Medium merchant convoys	15 knots, Fast
Hamburg ...	Yarmouth ...	323	...	32	$21\frac{1}{2}$
Bremen ...	,, ...	308	...	31	$20\frac{1}{2}$
Bremerhaven ...	,, ...	274	...	$27\frac{1}{2}$	18
Cuxhaven ...	,, ...	271	...	27	18
Wilhelmshaven ...	,, ...	263	...	26	$17\frac{1}{2}$
Amsterdam ... / Ijmuiden ...	} Lowestoft ...	102 from Ijmuiden	...	10 *Add* $\frac{1}{2}$ to 2 hrs. for docking, etc. *Add* 2 hrs. from Amsterdam	7 + $\frac{1}{2}$ to 2, + 2 from Amsterdam.
Rotterdam (Hook)	Southwold ...	92 from the Hook	$15\frac{1}{2}$ + 3–4 hrs. from Rotterdam	9 + 1–2 hrs. from Rotterdam	6 + 1 to 2 from Rotterdam.
Flushing ...	N. Foreland ...	{ 80	} $13\frac{1}{2}$ to 14	8–$8\frac{1}{2}$	$5\frac{1}{2}$
Antwerp ...	Orfordness ...	84 from Flushing }			
Ostend ...	Orfordness ...	71	12	7	5
	Deal ...	57	$9\frac{1}{2}$	$5\frac{1}{2}$	4
Dunkirk ...	Dungeness ...	53	9	5	$3\frac{1}{2}$
	Dover ...	38	$6\frac{1}{2}$	4	$2\frac{1}{2}$
Calais ...	Dover ...	21	$3\frac{1}{2}$	2	$1\frac{1}{2}$
	St. Margarets Bay	20	$3\frac{1}{2}$	2	$1\frac{1}{4}$
Boulogne ...	Folkestone ...	26	4	$2\frac{1}{2}$	$1\frac{3}{4}$
	Dungeness ...	26	4	$2\frac{1}{2}$	$1\frac{3}{4}$
Havre ...	Selsey ... / Little-hampton	80	$13\frac{1}{2}$	8	$5\frac{1}{2}$
,, ...	Newhaven ... / Eastbourne ...	76	13	$7\frac{1}{2}$	5
Cherbourg ...	Swanage ...	57	$9\frac{1}{2}$	6	4
Brest ...	Lizard ...	117	...	12	8
	Swanage ...	180	...	18	12
	Portsmouth ...	210	...	21	14
		To Ireland		Eng. Ire.	Eng. Ire.
Lorient ...	Lizard ...	193 336	...	19 $33\frac{1}{2}$	13 $22\frac{1}{2}$
St. Nazaire (Nantes)	,, ...	211 395	...	21 $49\frac{1}{2}$	14 26
La Rochelle ...	,, ...	318 462	...	32 46	21 $30\frac{1}{2}$
La Pallice (mouth of River).	,, ...	364 480	...	$36\frac{1}{2}$ 48	24 32
Bayonne ...	,, ...	423 566	...	42 $56\frac{1}{2}$	28 $37\frac{1}{2}$
Narvik	Reyjavik ...	1,094	...	109	73
	Scapa ...	813	...	81	54
	Yarmouth ...	1,086	...	109	72
Trondheim	Yarmouth ...	767	...	$76\frac{1}{2}$	51
	Scapa ...	515	...	51	34
	Reyjavik ...	985	...	$98\frac{1}{2}$	66
Kristiansand(S)	Yarmouth ...	400	...	40	27
	Scapa... ...	354	...	$35\frac{1}{2}$	$22\frac{1}{2}$

In arriving at both distances and time no allowance has been made for tide or navigational or mining hazards.

Only an approximation can be given for the time necessary to clear port and form station. In general 200 barges may be expected to need 1½ hours minimum if any formation is to be established. Many, however, could leave simultaneously, especially from ROTTERDAM, FLUSHING, HAVRE and CHERBOURG.

Merchant vessels will leave port at an average rate of 6 per hour except at CHERBOURG and BREST, where this rate would be considerably improved upon.

6 knots appears the most likely speed for barges, but it is improbable that they would be used for a passage of any considerable length.

APPENDIX XXIX

POSSIBLE DISTRIBUTION OF INVASION CRAFT AT CHANNEL PORTS, etc., FOR INVASION

(based on availability shown in Appendix IV, Table 2)

Ports	T.L.C.	Medium Barges	Small Barges	Dumb Barges	Tugs.	Siebel Ferries.
TEXEL	20	...	...	...	...	...
IJMUIDEN ...	225	...	...	...	...	...
HOOK	235	...	...	...	...	...
SCHELDT	...	...	...	1,000	1,000	...
ZEEBRUGGE ...	...	300 (300)(*a*)	...	...	50	...
OSTENDE	10	450 (300)	300	...	50	...
DUNKIRK ...	40	790 (445)	150	...	15	50
CALAIS	40	305 (200)	80	...	12	25
BOULOGNE ...	15	115	140	...	15	30
DIEPPE	40	250	...	...	...	...
FECAMP	30	70	30	...	6	30
HAVRE	140	720 (500)	240	...	12	25
CHERBOURG ...	...	...	...	...	...	...
Total	795	3,000 (1,745)	940	1,000	1,160	160

(*a*) Reserve barges retained in rear of the ports, but included in total of 3,000.

APPENDIX XXX

INVASION PORTS

Enemy Activity and Port Facilities

1. *DELFZIJL.*

A commercial port of some importance on the Ems Estuary.

Commercial shipping is in excess of peace-time standards. The port is constantly full of shipping, and with ROTTERDAM ranks as one of the principal ports now being used by Germany.

Damage by demolition in May, 1940, was probably slight, and the port is now apparently fully usable.

2. *DEN HELDER.*

A Dutch naval and shipbuilding base.

Little merchant shipping. A base for E boats and patrol craft. Storage units and ex-Dutch repair yards.

It is believed the Dutch destroyed much of the machinery and plant, but by now repairs have probably been effected.

3. *AMSTERDAM.*

Of less commercial importance than ROTTERDAM, handling about 5,000 ships a year and connected to the North Sea by the NORTH SEA CANAL to IJMUIDEN. Commercial shipping is reduced to a bare minimum of small vessels and barges.

Shipbuilding, however, is continuing. Yards are also busy on repairs and barge building.

4. *IJMUIDEN.*

Used as an E boat flotilla base and for a large number of fishing craft. There is only slight barge traffic.

Considerable silting up of the harbour must have occurred since 1940.

5. *ROTTERDAM.*

The largest Dutch port for liners, merchant ships and barges. There are dry docks and building slips for warships, submarines and liners. About 10,000 ships a year were handled in peace-time.

It is noteworthy that, of the Dutch, Belgian and French Channel ports, ROTTERDAM and DELFZIJL are being used for practically all large-scale commercial traffic.

Is a terminal point for convoys to and from Germany and Scandinavia, and considerable use is made of ROTTERDAM for internal barge traffic (possibly even for oil and ammunition), small tankers, merchant ships and coasters. About 800-1,000 barges are usually present.

There are eleven dockside storage units.

Its naval use is limited to E or R boats and patrol craft.

The shipbuilding yards are busy on naval and merchant shipping, and repair work, barge-building and conversion work is also being done.

Although the town was severely bombed by the Germans, the port facilities are not seriously affected.

6. *FLUSHING.*

A Dutch naval base with a small dry dock. Of small commercial importance in peace-time, except for cross-Channel traffic.

There is often quite a large volume of ships, barges and small craft at anchor in the roads, and this was particularly noticeable in September, 1940.

The locks and port facilities were severely damaged in May, 1940, but by September, 1940, the port had been restored to use.

7. *ANTWERP.*

One of the world's great ports, handling about 10,000 ships a year, and with practically unlimited capacity. A normal complement would be 200 ships and 1,000 barges. It is linked to the inland canals of Belgium, N.E. France, Switzerland and West Germany.

There is little activity in any class of traffic, either merchant or naval; only patrol craft use it. Distribution from ANTWERP is chiefly by rail, whereas it is by water from ROTTERDAM, and this may account for its decline in use.

On the other hand, from the military point of view, there is considerable evidence that the port was intended to be one of the main bases for operations against the U.K. in 1940. The continuation of practices in loading and unloading, an increase in ammunition storage and other factors emphasize the potential importance of this port in any future operations against the U.K.

Shipyards are active, both with ship and barge construction and barge conversion.

The damage to the docks by demolition may not yet be entirely repaired, but the port is considered fully usable.

8. *OSTEND.*

Cross-Channel port with extensive wet basins, and the outlet of the BRUGES-OSTEND Canal.

In September, 1940, OSTEND was used by the Germans as a barge-distribution port. Considerable construction of concrete shelters and ammunition units.

Used to a very limited extent by coasters, small craft, an occasional tanker and a minimum of barge traffic. E and R boats use the port.

Damage by demolition, bombing and shelling is extensive, but actual lock gates appear intact, and the port must be considered as usable, even if manual operation is necessary.

9. *DUNKIRK.*

Well-equipped cross-channel, commercial and barge port, but the canals connecting to it are small. It has extensive quays, wet basins and four dry docks.

Blockships remain in position, limiting traffic to small craft only, and the port remains practically inactive.

There was great barge activity in September, 1940.

Considerable concrete storage constructed early in 1941.

10. *CALAIS.*

A cross-channel and moderate commercial port, with extensive quayage.

Nothing of naval significance has been observed here for a considerable period; movements of even the smaller units have been very restricted.

The railway, town and port damage in June, 1940, was considerable. In spite of this and subsequent air bombardment, the port must now be considered usable.

11. *BOULOGNE.*

Principally a cross-channel and fishing port.

Except for E boats and patrol craft, it is little used. Some barges have remained in the Bassin Loubet since September, 1940, when very large numbers were present.

Much damage was effected by demolition and bombing, and it is probable the inner part of the harbour is still tidal. The port is, however, usable.

12. *DIEPPE.*

A cross-channel port with good quayage, repair yards and a dry dock.

The blockship and five other sunken ships still remain in position, and only small ships can enter. The port is not used for merchant shipping or naval craft, and no constructional activity has been seen.

13. *LE HAVRE.*

The outlet port for the Seine valley with a heavy peace-time trade. The TANCARVILLE Canal forms a sheltered route to the sea for barges.

HAVRE has been little used since June, 1940, but barges use the port and the TANCARVILLE Canal. Patrol boats use HAVRE, but not in any great quantity.

The port has received heavy damage, but the docks seem usable.

14. *ROUEN.*

The principal oil-importing port of France in peace-time.

Limited amount of merchant shipping, tanker traffic and barge activity.

15. *CHERBOURG.*

Principally a transatlantic liner port and naval base with building yards.

Is terminal port for convoys from Germany and Holland, and has been used as a base for torpedo boats and E boats.

Underground storage units at the Darse Transatlantique have been built and covered over.

Dockyards, buildings and the oil-pumping station (Darse Transatlantique) have been damaged by bombing.

16. *ST. MALO.*

A peace-time tourist, cross-channel, coastal traffic and fishing port, but entirely dependent on its tidal locks. It is also the main port for the CHANNEL ISLANDS.

Considerable damage was done to the lock gates in June, 1940. Repairs have been effected, as the main dock is now used. The port is used by patrol vessels and mine-sweepers.

There are some small yards at ST. MALO which are reported as busy, and are probably used for repairs.

17. *BREST.*

Primarily a naval base, with dry docks and building slips.

With its secure entrance and extensive dry docks, it has become the German West Coast base for battle cruisers, cruisers, destroyers, and more recently U boats. It is likely greater use will be made of it for U boats, as five shelter pens or docks are being built, with two-storied store and repair shops adjoining them. The commercial dry dock has been lengthened, and a new large dry dock is being excavated. Storage units have been built, and the jetty at the torpedo-boat station end widened.

Extensive use is made of netting booms, camouflage, and smoke screens to protect ships.

There is a small amount of tanker traffic. E and R boats and trawlers use the port occasionally.

Work at the seaplane base suggests greater use of it in the future.

18. *LORIENT.*

Has become a principal U boat base, full use being made of the dry docks and radial slips. Seven or eight are usually in port at one time, and the facilities are being increased.

Apart from a few coasters and fishing craft, there is no merchant ship traffic. R boats and armed trawlers are also based there.

19. *KEROMAN.*

Is one of the principal fishing and refrigerating centres of France. There is little merchant shipping activity, but submarine facilities are being increased.

20. *ST. NAZAIRE.*

One of the principal commercial ports of France.

Increasing use is being made of the port facilities, particularly for tankers, U boats and patrol craft. Coasters and merchant ships use the port, but not in great numbers. It is also used as a base for raider and U boat supply ships.

21. *NANTES.*

Important commercial port.

Little naval activity, but increasingly used by tankers and merchant ships chiefly of coastal type. It is possible it may develop as a terminal port for the iron ore trade from Spain.

22. *LA ROCHELLE.*

Is being used for merchant ships, coasters and fishing craft. It has facilities which may be used in the future for small naval craft.

23. *LA PALLICE.*

A commercial port with special facilities for discharging oil tankers. The port is being used by coasters and tankers, destroyers, patrol craft and occasional U boats. Work is proceeding on submarine shelters in the wet basin, and the main landing jetty is being completed.

24. *BORDEAUX.*

One of the principal commercial ports of France, with dry dock and shipbuilding yards.

There is a fairly constant merchant ship tonnage present of about 150,000 tons, and a fair, but not large, turnover of shipping.

It has been principally developed as the Italian submarine base, but German destroyers and patrol craft have also used it.

APPENDIX XXXI

WINTER CONDITIONS IN INVASION PORTS

Ports	Remarks regarding the likelihood of ports being closed by ice.
NARVIK TRONDHEIM BERGEN STAVANGER Other small ports in SKAGGERAK (NORWAY) KRISTIANSAND, S. ARENDAL LARVIK	Never closed.
DRAMMEN OSLO	Heads of fjords only are closed perhaps once in 10 years for, say, 5 weeks in late February and March.
STETTIN	Closed for perhaps 3 weeks in an exceptionally severe winter.
STRALSUND ROSTOCK WISMAR LUBECK KIEL	Closed perhaps twice in 10 years for one to four weeks from early February to mid-March.
BREMEN BREMERHAVEN WILHELMSHAVEN CUXHAVEN	Never likely to be closed.
BRUNSBUTTEL EMDEN	Closed for perhaps three weeks in February in exceptional winter such as 1940-41.
HAMBURG	Closed for up to four weeks in exceptional winter between end of January and early March.
DEN HELDER	In a severe winter like 1940-41, may be closed for, say, two weeks in February.
IJMUIDEN AMSTERDAM ROTTERDAM	Even in a severe winter these ports can be kept open by ice-breaker.
ANTWERP ESBJERG (W. JUTLAND)	Never closed.

APPENDIX XXXII

ARTILLERY OF GERMAN FIELD FORMATIONS (*See* footnote)

Serial No. (a)	Calibre and Nomenclature (b)	Type of Weapon (c)	Weight of Projectile (d)	Rate of Fire r.p.m. (e)	Weight in Action (f)	Maximum Range yds. (g)	Remarks (h)
A 1	7·92 mm. (0·31 in.) (Pz. B. 39)	A. Tk. rifle 39	0·52 ozs.	6-8 single shot	...	...	Fires A.P. or A.P. lachrymatory bullets with cemented carbide core.
2	2 cm. (0·79 in.) (Solothurn)	A. Tk. rifle ...	5·5 ozs.	10-20 single shot	110 lbs.	...	Fires A.P.
A T 3	2 cm. (0·79 in.) (2 cm. Flak 30)	Super heavy A.A/A.Tk. M.G.	4·0 ozs. H.E. 5·3 ozs. A.P.	120-150	1,036 lbs.	6,150 horizontal 4,050 vertical	Fires A.P. dual purpose A.A./A.Tk.
A 4	2 cm. (0·79 in.) (Pz. B. 41)	A. Tk. gun, model 41	1·78 ozs.	8-10	500 lbs.	...	Fires special projectile with cemented carbide A.P. coil.
A T 5	3·7 cm. (1·46 in.) (3·7 cm. Pak)	A. Tk. gun ...	1·68 lbs.	8-10	748 lbs.	...	Fires normal A.P., special A.P. 40 or H.E.
	3·7 cm. (3·7 cm. Flak)	A.A. gun ...	1·43 lbs.	80-100	1·69 tons	...	
T 6	4·7 cm. (1·85 in.) (4·7 cm. Pak)	S.P. A.Tk. gun	3·75 lbs.	...	7·5 tons	...	Fires normal or special A.P. 40 or H.E. on Pz. Kw. I (5·7-ton) tank chassis.
T 7	5 cm. (1·97 in.) (5 cm. Kw. K.)	Tank gun ...	4·56 lbs.	...	...	...	Fires normal or special A.P. or H.E. in Pz. Kw. III (18-ton) tank.
A 8	5 cm. (1·97 in.) (5 cm. Pak 38)	A. Tk. gun, model 38	4·56 lbs.	...	...	...	Fires normal A.P., special A.P. 40 or H.E.

APPENDIX XXXII—*continued*

ARTILLERY OF GERMAN FIELD FORMATIONS—*continued*

Serial No.	Calibre and Nomenclature	Type of Weapon	Weight of Projectile	Rate of Fire r.p.m.	Weight in Action	Maximum Range yds.	Remarks
(*a*)	(*b*)	(*c*)	(*d*)	(*e*)	(*f*)	(*g*)	(*h*)
T 9	7·5 cm. (2·95 in.) (7·5 cm. Kw. K.)	Tank gun ...	15·13 lbs.	...	672 lbs.	...	Fires A.P., H.E. or smoke in Pz. Kw. IV (22-ton) tank, or on Pz. Kw. III chassis (*see* Serial 14).
10	8·8 cm. (3·46 in.) (8·8 cm. Flak 18)	A.A./A.Tk. gun	19·8 lbs.	12-15	5·07 tons	18,000 horizontal 39,400 ft. vertical	Fires A.P. or H.E. On S.P. mounting for engagement of ground targets.
A 11	7·5 cm. L.M.W. 18 (2·95 in.)	Infantry howitzer	12 lbs. 13·2 lbs.	...	·35 tons	3,860 3,780	
12	7·5 cm. L. Inf. G. L/13 (2·95 in.)	Infantry howitzer ...	10-14 lbs.	...	·37 tons	4,200-5,600	May not yet have been brought into use.
A 13	7·5 cm. Geb. K. 15 (2·95 in.)	Mountain gun	12 lbs.	...	·62 tons	5,900 7,250	
14	7·5 cm. Sturmgeschütz (2·95 in.)	S.P. assault gun	14 lbs.	...	...	9,000 yds.	Fires H.E., A.P. and smoke. This is the gun of Serial 9 mounted on armoured Pz. Kw. III chassis.
15	10·5 cm. L.F.H. 18 (4·13 in.)	Gun howitzer ...	32·6 lbs.	...	1·9 tons	11,640	Also fires A.P. and smoke.
16	10 cm. K. 18 (4·13 in.) (actual calibre 10·5 cm.)	Gun	35 lbs. ...	...	5·5 tons	19,700	

A 17	15 cm. S. Inf. G. 33 (5·91 in.)	Heavy infantry howitzer	80 lbs. ...	...	1·5 tons	6,000	
18	15 cm. Sturmgeschütz (5·91 in.)	S.P. assault gun	80 lbs.	...	...	6,000	Gun of Serial 17 mounted on armoured Pz. Kw. I chassis.
19	15 cm. S.F.H. 25 (t) (5·91 in.)	Howitzer ...	91 lbs. ...	...	3·68 tons	13,000	Skoda.
20	15 cm. S.F.H. 18 (5·9 in.)	Howitzer ...	95·7 lbs.	...	4·5 tons	16,400	
A 21	55 mm. ("5 cm.") (2·16 in.)	Mortar	2 lbs. ...	45 ...	30·8 lbs.	500	Fires H.E. One charge only.
A 22	81 mm. ("8 cm.") (3·2 in.)	Mortar	7·75 lbs.	44-45 ...	125 lbs. ...	2,100	Fires H.E. and smoke. Four charges.
A 23	120 mm. ("12 cm.") Tampella (4·7 in.)	Mortar	27·5 lbs. (light) 47·3 lbs. (heavy)	12 ...	562 lbs. ...	7,500 (light bomb) 4,900 (heavy bomb)	Fires light and heavy H.E. Five charges.

Weapons marked A may be airborne.
Weapons marked T may be mounted on tanks which could be landed on beaches from T.L.C., etc.

APPENDIX XXXIII

SUPPLIES FOR GERMAN DIVISIONS IN OPERATIONS AGAINST U.K.

1. It is estimated that a British division requires 200 tons per day for supplies of food, ammunition, petrol and lubricants. This figure covers bare minimum requirements of a division and does not allow for the considerable amount of extra stores (*e.g.*, R.E. and ordnance) which would be required for even a short campaign. The total approximate tonnage required for the maintenance of a British division is 350 tons per day.

2. It is estimated that for a short campaign the Germans would attempt to land during the first 10 days a maximum of 300 tons per day per division, this figure to include an allowance for corps and army troops as well as an engineer stores required for the provision and repair of landing facilities.

3. It is estimated that the troops in the main seaborne attack would require approximately a daily total of 9,000 tons. Casualties would reduce this figure, but on the other hand the airborne troops would also require supplies.

4. 8-10,000 tons, therefore, appears to be a fair estimate.

APPENDIX XXXIV

ESTIMATED DAILY CAPACITY OF PORTS (THE WASH TO WEYMOUTH) FOR UNLOADING GENERAL CARGO, USING FULL EXISTING FACILITIES.

KING'S LYNN	2,000 tons.
GREAT YARMOUTH	1,000 tons.
LOWESTOFT	750 tons.
IPSWICH	3,000 tons.
COLCHESTER...	600 tons.
LONDON (P.L.A. Area)	Unlimited.
ROCHESTER	1,500 tons.
RAMSGATE	500 tons.*
DOVER	1,000 tons.*
FOLKESTONE...	200 tons.*
NEWHAVEN	500 tons.*
SHOREHAM	500 tons.
LITTLEHAMPTON	1,000 tons.
SOUTHAMPTON	25,000 tons.
POOLE	3,000 tons.
WEYMOUTH	500 tons.

Notes.

1. These estimates are based on wharfage available at date, and are approximate only.

2. In considering the capacity available to the enemy, allowance must be made for the elaborate precautions taken to neutralize the above ports should they be likely to fall into enemy hands.

3. Ports marked * are already partially immobilized.

4. PORTSMOUTH and HARWICH, being naval harbours, would only be suitable for unloading stores and light vehicles.

APPENDIX XXXV

PORTS IN EIRE

1. The following ports in Eire are considered the most likely for the Germans to attempt to use:—

CORK WATERFORD LIMERICK	Major landings.
GALWAY WESTPORT SLIGO DONEGAL BAY	Minor landings.

2. Ports in ST. GEORGE'S CHANNEL and the IRISH SEA are unlikely to be selected, owing to their proximity to our own naval and air bases.

3. A revision of the figures of the capacity of the ports in Eire for unloading troops, M.T. and guns is in course of preparation.

APPENDIX XXXVI

CAPACITY OF THE PORTS AND BEACHES BETWEEN NORTH FORELAND AND DUNGENESS.

N.B.—It is assumed that every port and beach will be used to maximum capacity.

1. *Ports.*

The ports available to the enemy are:—

RAMSGATE,
DOVER.
FOLKESTONE.

These ports have already been partially immobilized. In estimating their capacity for supplying the enemy the following assumptions have been made:—

(*a*) Enemy ships would have to unload by means of their own derricks.

(*b*) The ports would be in a damaged condition, but the blockages, etc., at harbour entrances would have been removed by the enemy.

(*c*) The Germans would not have obtained sufficient local air superiority to prevent the Royal Air Force from interfering substantially with German unloading operations. It is estimated that such interference would reduce handling capacity by at least fifty per cent.

(*d*) Sufficient transport and personnel would have been landed before the arrival of the supply ships to clear the supplies from the quay sides.

Upon the above assumptions, and taking into consideration the degree of immobilization that the ports will have suffered, the maximum capacity of the three ports per day of 24 hours is estimated at:—

	Initial Stages.	*After 7 days.*
RAMSGATE	50 tons	200 tons
DOVER	150 tons	800 tons
FOLKESTONE	150 tons	600 tons

2. *Beaches.*

In considering the places at which supplies are likely to be landed, attention has been directed primarily to the beaches and their exits; the only continuous stretch of beach suitable for landing supplies in large quantities and providing exits to forward communications lies between two miles east of DUNGENESS and SANDGATE—a distance of approximately 13 miles. Other parts of the beach between DUNGENESS and NORTH FORELAND, such as PEGWELL BAY and ST. MARGARET-AT-CLIFFE, where only very limited quantities of stores might be landed, have not been included either because of unsuitability of the foreshore or lack of forward communication.

In preparing the estimate the following assumptions have been made:—

(*a*) The Germans would not have obtained sufficient local air superiority to prevent the Royal Air Force from interfering substantially with German unloading operations. It is believed that such interference would reduce handling capacity by at least fifty per cent.

(*b*) The enemy would employ Dutch skoots or motor barges each capable of carrying 250 tons of military stores which would be run ashore at high water.

(*c*) Sufficient transport, beach material and personnel would have been landed (before the arrival of the supply barges) to clear supplies from the beaches on arrival.

(*d*) All beach defences would have been removed or rendered useless.

(*e*) Not more than four barges per mile would be beached. It is considered that any greater density would involve such congestion as to render the clearance of the stores impracticable.

Each barge could probably unload 100 tons of military supplies per 12-hour working day. Along the stretch of 13 miles of beach above referred to 52 barges could, therefore, unload simultaneously, and a total of 5,200 tons of military stores could be unloaded in a 12-hours working day.

This estimate of the capacity of the beaches is not based on experience, of which there is none available, but an exercise in combined operations has provided some evidence.

3. *Conclusions.*

Upon the assumptions set out above it is estimated that the maximum daily total of supplies which the Germans could land in the area between NORTH FORELAND and DUNGENESS would be:—

	Initial Stages.	*After 7 days.*
(*a*) Through the ports ...	350	1,600
(*b*) Through the beaches ...	5,200	6,800
Total	5,550	6,800

The maximum would be exceedingly difficult to attain. Any substantial destruction that could be effected on the enemy line of supply, sea communications, exits from the beaches and road communications by the Royal Navy, the Royal Air Force and long range guns must greatly reduce this figure. Moreover, the German ground defences against air attack in the early stages of their operations would not be fully developed.

APPENDIX XXXVII

TIDAL CONDITIONS ON EAST AND SOUTH COASTS

1. It is a widely held opinion that the enemy would prefer to land at dawn on a rising tide, not long before high water, that is to say on a day when high water occurs an hour or two after dawn.

2. Since high water occurs at different times along the coast, the enemy cannot benefit from these conditions at all his landing places, if he wants to land at dawn at all points. Between SELSEY BILL and ORFORDNESS this time difference between places is small. Between ORFORDNESS and the WASH it is considerable.

3. Thus on 6 April, 1941, dawn was about 0500 and high water occurred:—

SELSEY BILL (double tides) at 0624 and 0722
DOVER 0631
ORFORDNESS 0607
CROMER 0054

(All times British Summer Time.)

That is to say, on 6 April conditions would be good between SELSEY BILL and ORFORDNESS, but would rapidly become worse towards the North until they became bad at the WASH, where the landing would take place just before low water.

Good conditions would not obtain at CROMER till 11 April.

4. From purely tidal conditions, therefore, the best dates would be from 6 April extending to 11 April. These conditions repeat themselves fortnightly.

APPENDIX XXXVIII

FACTORS IN JANUARY, 1942, AFFECTING THE POSSIBILITY OF INVASION IN THE SPRING OF 1942

1. The Germans are committed to a major campaign on a front of 1,500 miles with substantially the whole of their first line forces engaged, and all their supply and transport arrangements directed to that front. From a military point of view it is inconceivable that they could break off that offensive without first achieving a major objective either as the result of the defeat or capitulation of the Russian in the field or by making such territorial gains as would preclude the possibility of future counter-action by the Russian forces.

2. Air superiority is a prerequisite of a successful invasion, and is probably recognized as such by Germany. One of the effects of the Russian Campaign is that Germany's air strength must have suffered considerable wastage. This, coupled with our own increased air strength, renders it impossible, particularly as regards fighters, for Germany to obtain such superiority by the spring.

3. Calculations show that Germany could not after the dislocation and wastage of the Russian Campaign withdraw, re-equip and re-group air forces for full scale invasion operations against this country in less than six to eight weeks after the withdrawal from Russia had begun.

4. Similarly Germany could not withdraw six or more armoured divisions from Russia, refit them, re-group them and concentrate them for embarkation for an invasion of this country in less than six to eight weeks after she had been able to begin her withdrawal from Russia. She should be able to make the necessary infantry available within this time.

5. Our increasing air strength in the Middle East will probably cause Germany to reinforce her air forces there at the earliest possible moment for the protection of her shipping routes from the Black Sea and to support her land forces.

6. Our improved reconnaissance facilities have increased our ability to obtain warning of the enemy's intentions and to bomb enemy shipping and concentrations in invasion ports. Similarly, our increased fighter strength will enable us to continue to bomb the nearer ports in daylight.

7. Our bombing of Germany's shipping is reducing the margin of shipping available for purposes of invasion.

8. The defences of this country have been strengthened and our army for home defence is becoming progressively better equipped and trained.

9. At sea we are stronger than in September, 1940, in craft suitable for repelling invasion.

10. Germany's communication problem in Russia, added to that in Europe as a whole, would be increased by the further commitment of an attempted invasion. Continued interference by bombing of Germany's transportation system would delay concentration for invasion.

11. Germany is still building invasion craft and carrying out invasion exercises. It cannot, therefore, be supposed that she has abandoned for all time the intention to invade. In any case she will have obvious reasons for maintaining the threat.

APPENDIX XXXIX

WEATHER CONDITIONS IN PERIOD SEPTEMBER-MAY IN RELATION TO INVASION

1. *General.*

It may be said that as the days shorten the weather becomes more disturbed, and stormy conditions begin to assert themselves after those of summer, which may be considered to end at a date, varying from year to year, between the second and third week in September and second week in October. Spells of quiet weather occur with decreasing frequency during the period September-January.

2. The average number of occasions during the months of September-May on which spells of weather *of at least four days' duration suitable for landing operations* have occurred during the last ten years is shown in the accompanying table.

SUITABLE WEATHER SPELLS

Month	Average number of four-day spells				
	East Scotland	East England	South England	West Ireland	Irish Sea
September	4·9	3·9	4·3	2·3	2·5
October	3·3	3·0	2·2	1·1	1·1
November	2·8	2·7	2·2	1·4	1·4
December	3·5	3·1	2·9	1·8	1·7
January	2·3	2·1	1·8	1·1	1·1
February	2·3	1·9	1·7	1·7	1·3
March	2·8	2·0	2·3	1·3	1·8
April	3·4	2·2	2·7	1·9	1·9
May	5·0	3·3	4·5	1·9	3·1

3. *Explanation of Table.*

3.0 spells for East Coast of England in October means that there is an average of 12 days of suitable weather which may, however, be in one spell or may be subdivided, *e.g.*, into spells of four and eight days; it must, however, be borne in mind that, in fact, there may be one spell of say 20 days in any one year and no spell of four days or more in the next year.

Suitable weather is assessed to be wind of not more than force four (12½-17 m.p.h.) blowing on shore, or not more than force five (18½-23 m.p.h.) blowing off shore. A wind of force five would, however, be too great for small craft in the open sea.

As the prevailing winds are westerly there is a larger number of favourable spells for the east coasts of England and Scotland than elsewhere, owing to the break caused by the land.

4. *Deductions from Investigation of Conditions for the Years* 1930-39 (*incl.*).

It seems that a suitable spell on the south and east coasts is more likely during December than in either November, January or February.

There is not invariably a quiet spell of four days in April on the south coast of England, but in May there was not one year without a spell of at least six days. It is also of interest that there appears greater likelihood of suitable conditions during the Spring on the south coast of England and east coast of Scotland than on the east coast of England.

5. *Wind.*

W.S.W is the predominant wind direction throughout the year, though north-easterly winds increase slightly in frequency in October and November, and become nearly as frequent as westerlies in April and May on the east coasts.

Land and sea breezes are appreciable in fair weather in the months of May to September, and result in a larger proportion of on-shore winds during the afternoons, and of light off-shore winds or calms at night and early morning.

Gales, usually westerly, are about thrice as numerous in October and four times as numerous in November as in September. Winds of force three and under are nearly twice as frequent in September as in November, while October comes nearer the latter than the former. During the winter months gales are a little more frequent than in November, as many as 17 in January, the worst month, being probable somewhere in the British Isles. In March the frequency falls off, 10 gales a month to be expected, and in May the chances are small.

6. *Visibility.*

Sea fog, *i.e.,* poor visibility of fairly uniform thickness over most of the English Channel is uncommon in any of the months September-March, and occurs on perhaps one and a half days a month.

In quiet and settled weather with clear skies at night, fog is liable to form over the land, particularly between November and March, but this is unlikely to spread far out to sea in November, and less likely in September and October. It is most likely to occur on the south-east coast, and is least likely in the west and north.

During favourable spells in November, two days in nine on the east coast of England are likely to be foggy, whereas in September foggy days amount to one day in twenty.

Fog has accompanied spells of quiet weather more often in December than in November, January or February, and, as in autumn, more often in S.E. and E. England (where it occurs on at least one day in four during these spells) than on the other coasts.

Fog over the land becomes less frequent after February, and is comparatively uncommon from April onwards, but fog at sea, particularly off east and south-east England and east Scotland becomes increasingly frequent in May.

7. *Low Cloud.*

Skies overcast with low cloud (including cloud below 1,000 feet) are increasingly more frequent towards winter, and there are more days with clear skies (or nearly so) in September than in the other autumn months.

Favourable spells in the September-November quarter are the least likely to be accompanied by 10/10ths low cloud on the south coast of England, the proportion of overcast days being about one day in four in E. England and on the western coasts, one day in seven in E. Scotland, and one in ten in S. England. These figures are much the same for each month of this quarter.

Of the winter months December to February, overcast days with low cloud are a little more frequent during quiet spells in December on the east and south coasts, where they amount to about a third of the otherwise suitable days.

Skies overcast with low cloud are infrequent during quiet spells in March-May except on the east coast of England, and to a less-marked extent the south coast of England and east coast of Scotland in May; these days are usually associated with north-easterly or easterly winds.

8. *Rain.*

October is the wettest month of the year on the south and east coasts of England, an appreciable fall being experienced on about ten days a month. November and December are nearly as wet as October, but September is considerably drier. January to March experience on the average about six days a month with sufficient rain to hamper operations, whereas April and May are usually the driest months of the year. In late December and in January and February, there is the additional risk, though small, of snow lying.

APPENDIX XL

LENGTH AND NATURE OF WARNING OF ATTACK LIKELY TO BE RECEIVED

Nature of warning	*Length of warning*
1. Withdrawal of submarines from the trade routes to protect invasion convoys.	About 3 weeks (time would be required for re-fitting).
2. A marked change in German air tactics involving—	
(*a*) a strong interference with our air reconnaissance;	9 to 10 days.
(*b*) marked intensification of bombing operations, or alternatively complete cessation;	9 to 10 days.
(*c*) attempts at renewal of bombing operations by day.	?
3. Increased activity at invasion ports and surrounding areas, and on the roads and railways leading to them, *e.g.*, large assemblies of M.T. and appearance of dumps.	Up to 9 days.
4. The return of G.A.F. units from other theatres of war and from Germany to North-West Europe, and in particular the return of dive-bombing units to the Channel coast area.	6 to 8 weeks. (*see* also Appendix XXXVIII).
5. The return from other theatres of war to North-West Europe of armoured and infantry formations.	6 to 8 weeks. (*see* also Appendix XXXVIII).
6. The withdrawal of transport aircraft from normal duties.	About a week.
7. Despatch of enemy heavy ships into the Atlantic in such a way as to draw off our main forces.	About 5 days.

Nature of warning	*Length of warning*
8. Alternatively, concentration of German heavy ships prior to their sailing.	A fleeting warning likely to occur not longer than 24 hours before sailing, if then.
9. Change of bombing targets to fighter defences, communications, ports, and the Fleet.	2 to 3 days.
10. Increase in W.T. traffic to the invasion port areas.	24 to 48 hours.
11. Extensive mining of naval harbours.	24 hours.

N.B.—The mere assembly of shipping and barges at the invasion ports is not likely to give any reliable indication of the actual date of sailing, as such assembly may be completed some time previous to the actual zero date.

APPENDIX XLI.

STATES OF READINESS—INVASION OF U.K.

1. *Navy.*

The Royal Navy has three states of readiness, as follows:—

3rd Degree of Readiness ...	The enemy is preparing for invasion, but attack is not expected in the next three days.
2nd Degree of Readiness ...	The enemy is in every respect prepared for invasion and it is considered likely that attack will take place in the next three days.
1st Degree of Readiness ...	Invasion is imminent and attack is likely to occur within the next 12 hours.

2. *R.A.F.*

The R.A.F. has three states of readiness as follows:—

Invasion Alert No. 3 ...	Attack is regarded as improbable within the following three days, although an invasion threat is believed to exist.
Invasion Alert No. 2 ...	Attack is regarded as probable within the following three days.
Invasion Alert No. 1 ...	Attack is regarded as imminent and likely to occur within the next 12 hours.

3. *Army.*

The Army has three states of readiness as follows:—

(*a*) NORMAL.

(*b*) STAND TO.

(*c*) ACTION STATIONS.

(*a*) " Normal " is that state of readiness which exists when invasion is considered unlikely in the immediate future, but raids are possible.

(*b*) " Stand to " is ordered when conditions are particularly favourable for invasion. It is a complete state of readiness to resist invasion for all regular troops, and for such Home Guard as Army Commanders may decide.

(*c*) " Action stations " is ordered when there is an immediate threat of invasion. It is a complete state of readiness to resist invasion, and the Home Guard is called out.

(B41/527) 1500 2/42 W.O.P. 9372 (*T.S. 10157*)

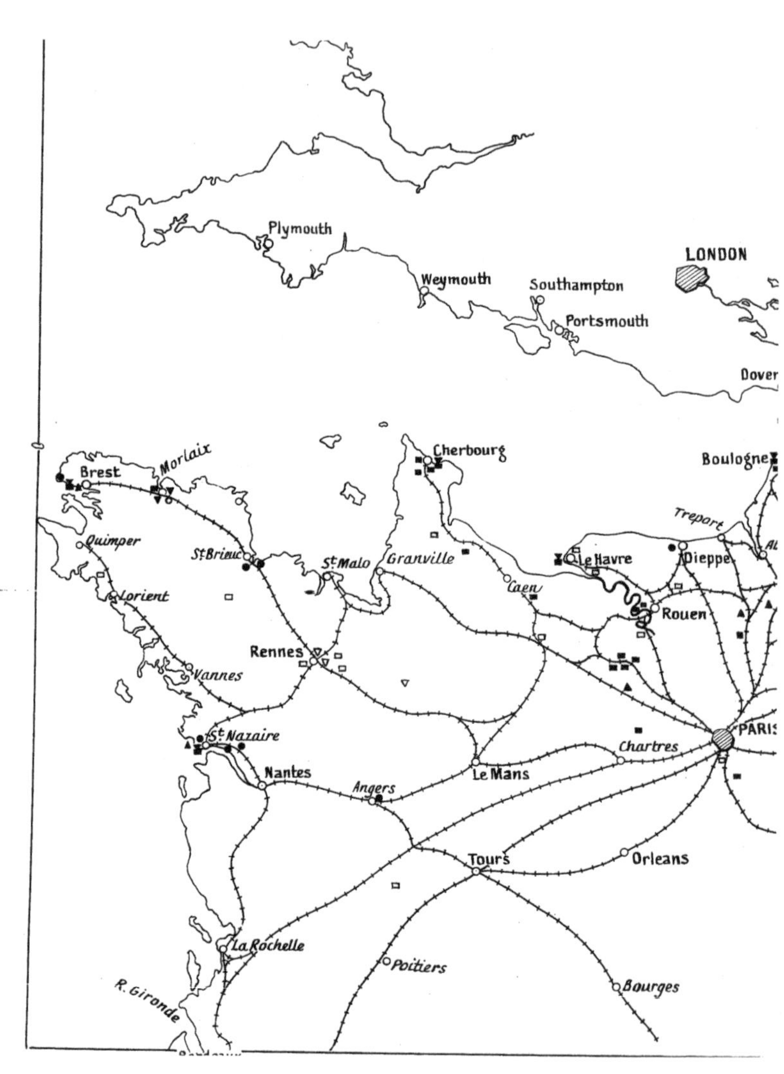
Plymouth
LONDON
Weymouth
Southampton
Portsmouth
Dover
Cherbourg
Boulogne
Brest
Morlaix
Treport
Quimper
St Brieuc
St Malo
Granville
Le Havre
Dieppe
Caen
Rouen
Lorient
Rennes
Vannes
PARIS
St Nazaire
Chartres
Nantes
Le Mans
Angers
Tours
Orleans
La Rochelle
Poitiers
Bourges
R. Gironde

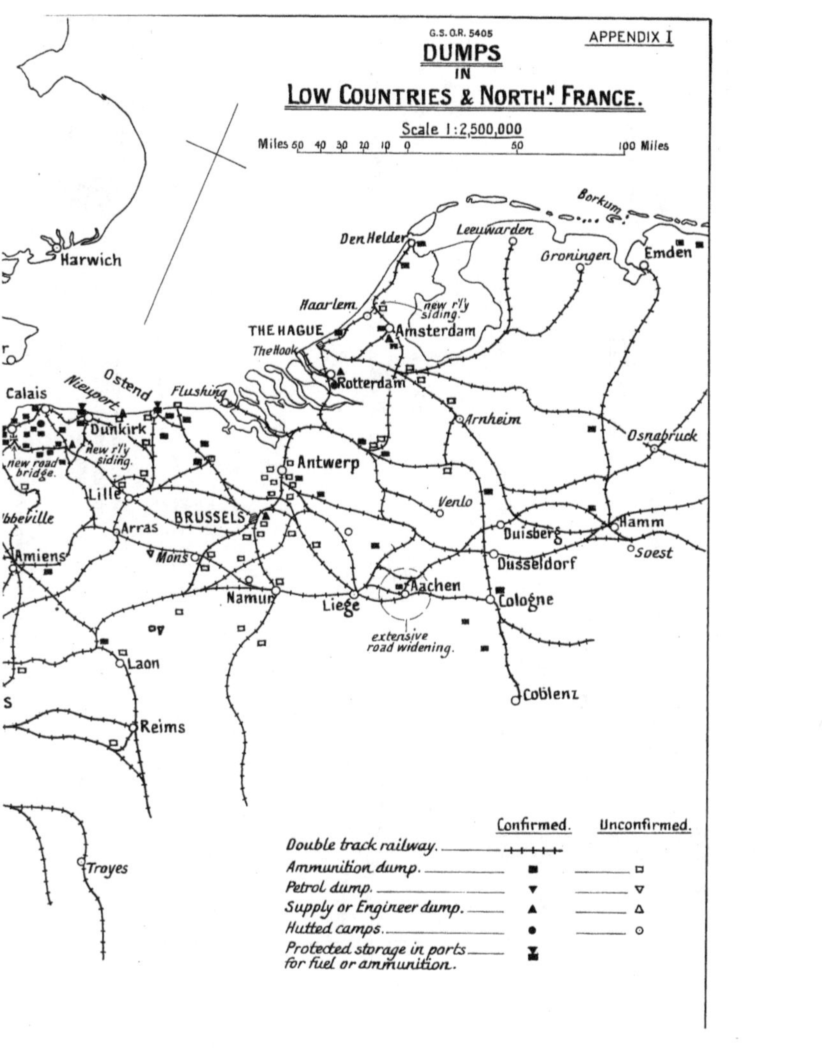
G.S.O.R. 5405
APPENDIX I
DUMPS
IN
LOW COUNTRIES & NORTHN. FRANCE.
Scale 1:2,500,000
Miles 50 40 30 20 10 0 50 100 Miles
Borkum
Den Helder
Leeuwarden
Groningen
Emden
Harwich
Haarlem
new r'ly siding.
THE HAGUE
Amsterdam
The Hook
Rotterdam
Calais
Nieuport
Ostend
Flushing
Dunkirk
new r'ly siding.
new road bridge.
Arnheim
Osnabruck
Antwerp
Lille
Venlo
Abbeville
Arras
BRUSSELS
Duisberg
Hamm
Soest
Amiens
Mons
Dusseldorf
Aachen
Namur
Liege
Cologne
extensive road widening.
Laon
Coblenz
Reims
Troyes
Confirmed.
Unconfirmed.
Double track railway.
Ammunition dump.
Petrol dump.
Supply or Engineer dump.
Hutted camps.
Protected storage in ports for fuel or ammunition.

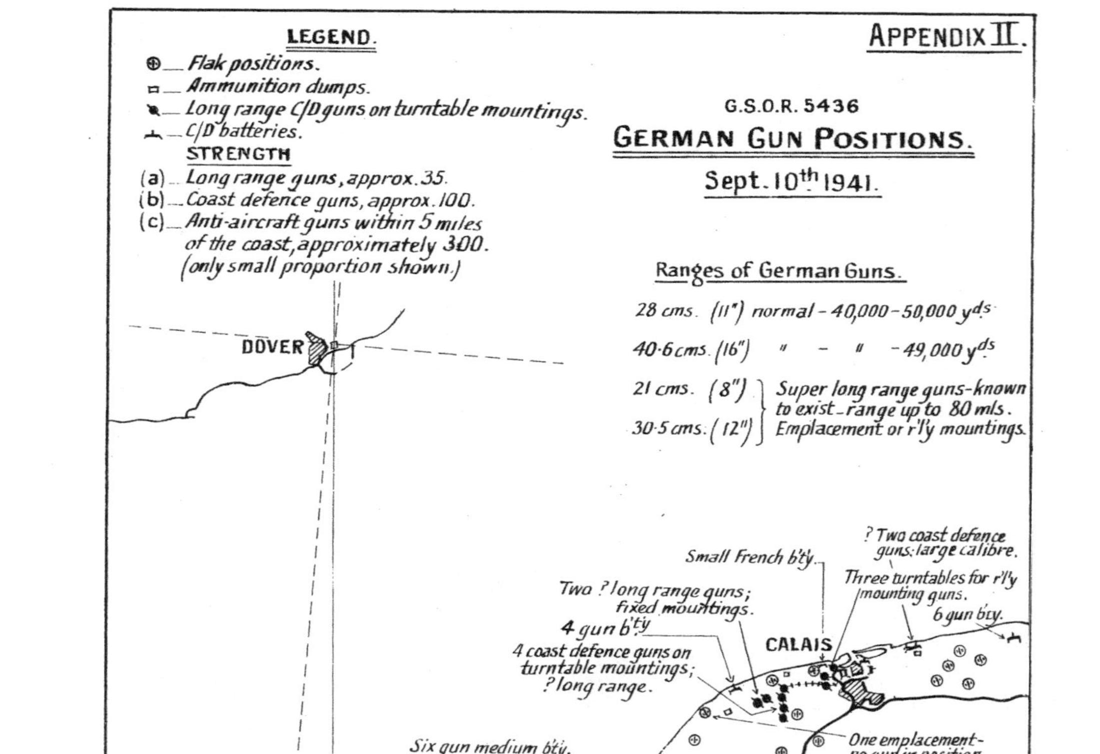
APPENDIX II.
LEGEND.
⊕ — Flak positions.
▫ — Ammunition dumps.
● — Long range C/D guns on turntable mountings.
⊥ — C/D batteries.
STRENGTH
(a) — Long range guns, approx. 35.
(b) — Coast defence guns, approx. 100.
(c) — Anti-aircraft guns within 5 miles of the coast, approximately 300. (only small proportion shown.)
G.S.O.R. 5436
GERMAN GUN POSITIONS.
Sept. 10th 1941.
Ranges of German Guns.
28 cms. (11") normal – 40,000–50,000 yds.
40·6 cms. (16") " – " – 49,000 yds.
21 cms. (8")
30·5 cms. (12")
Super long range guns – known to exist – range up to 80 mls. Emplacement or r'l'y mountings.
DOVER
CALAIS
Small French b'ty.
? Two coast defence guns; large calibre.
Three turntables for r'l'y mounting guns.
6 gun b'ty.
Two ? long range guns; fixed mountings.
4 gun b'ty.
4 coast defence guns on turntable mountings; ? long range.
Six gun medium b'ty.
One emplacement – no gun in position.

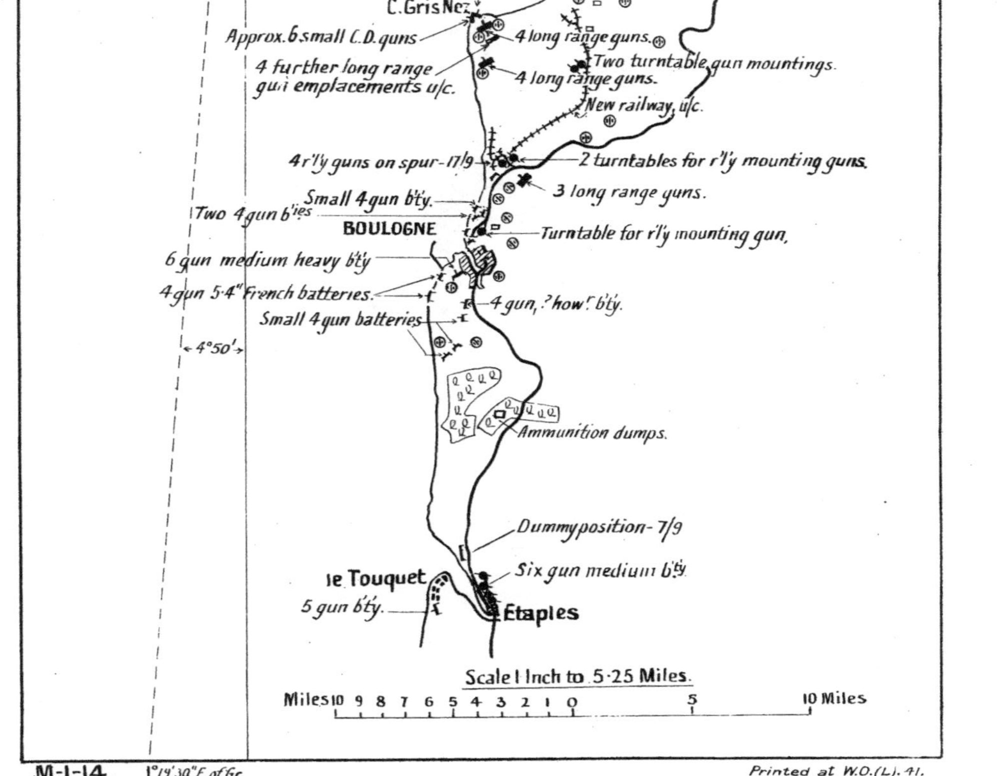
C. Gris Nez
Approx. 6 small C.D. guns
4 long range guns.
4 further long range gun emplacements u/c.
Two turntable gun mountings.
4 long range guns.
New railway, u/c.
4 r'l'y guns on spur - 17/9
2 turntables for r'l'y mounting guns.
3 long range guns.
Small 4 gun b'ty.
Two 4 gun b'ies
BOULOGNE
Turntable for r'l'y mounting gun,
6 gun medium heavy b'ty
4 gun 5·4" French batteries.
4 gun, ? how'. b'ty.
Small 4 gun batteries
4°50'
Ammunition dumps.
Dummy position - 7/9
Six gun medium b'ty
le Touquet
5 gun b'ty.
Etaples
Scale 1 Inch to 5·25 Miles.
Miles 10 9 8 7 6 5 4 3 2 1 0 5 10 Miles
M-1-14. 1°19'30" E. of Gr.

Printed at W.O.(L). 41.

APPENDIX V

1

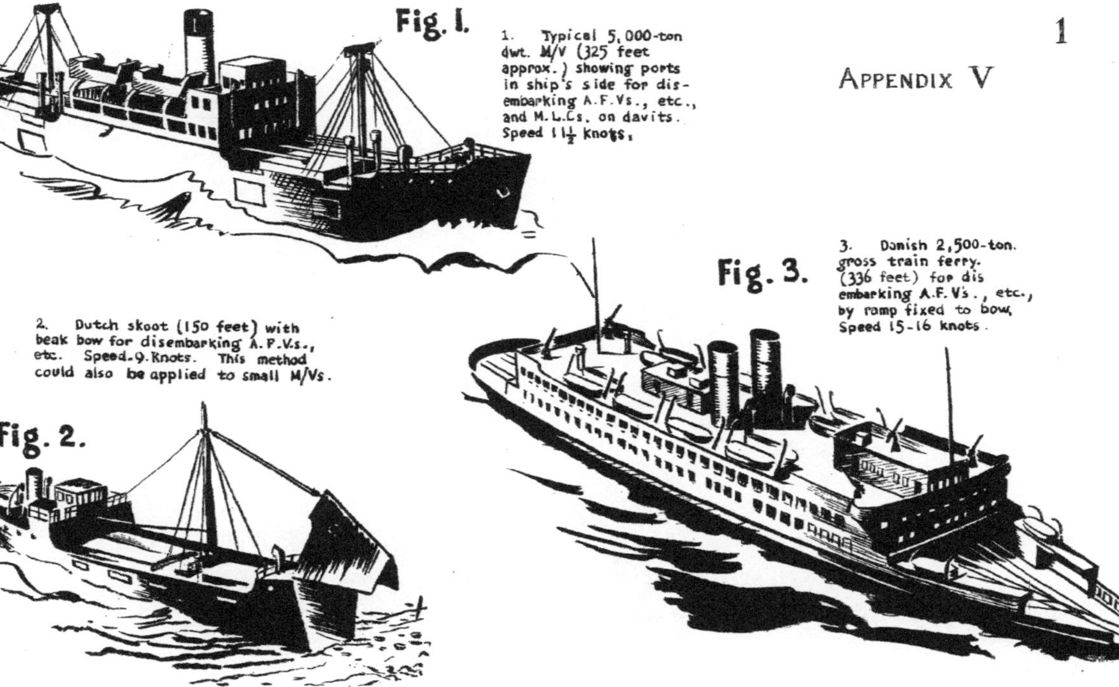

Fig. I.
1. Typical 5,000-ton dwt. M/V (325 feet approx.) showing ports in ship's side for disembarking A.F.Vs., etc., and M.L.Cs. on davits. Speed 11½ knots.
Fig. 2.
2. Dutch skoot (150 feet) with beak bow for disembarking A.F.Vs., etc. Speed 9 Knots. This method could also be applied to small M/Vs.
Fig. 3.
3. Danish 2,500-ton gross train ferry. (336 feet) for disembarking A.F.Vs., etc., by ramp fixed to bow, Speed 15-16 knots.

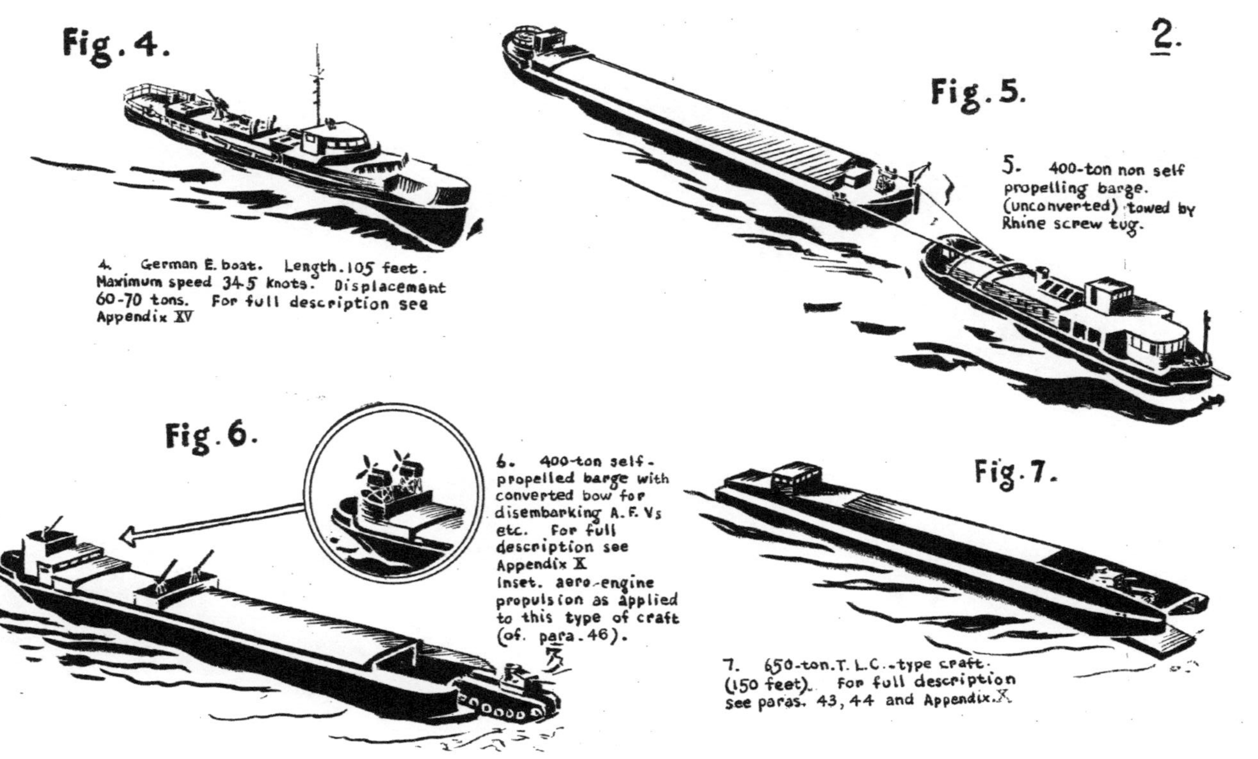

Fig. 4.

4. German E. boat. Length. 105 feet. Maximum speed 34.5 knots. Displacement 60-70 tons. For full description see Appendix XV

Fig. 5.

5. 400-ton non self propelling barge. (unconverted) towed by Rhine screw tug.

Fig. 6.

6. 400-ton self-propelled barge with converted bow for disembarking A. F. Vs etc. For full description see Appendix X
Inset. aero-engine propulsion as applied to this type of craft (of. para. 46).

Fig. 7.

7. 650-ton. T. L. C.-type craft. (150 feet). For full description see paras. 43, 44 and Appendix. X

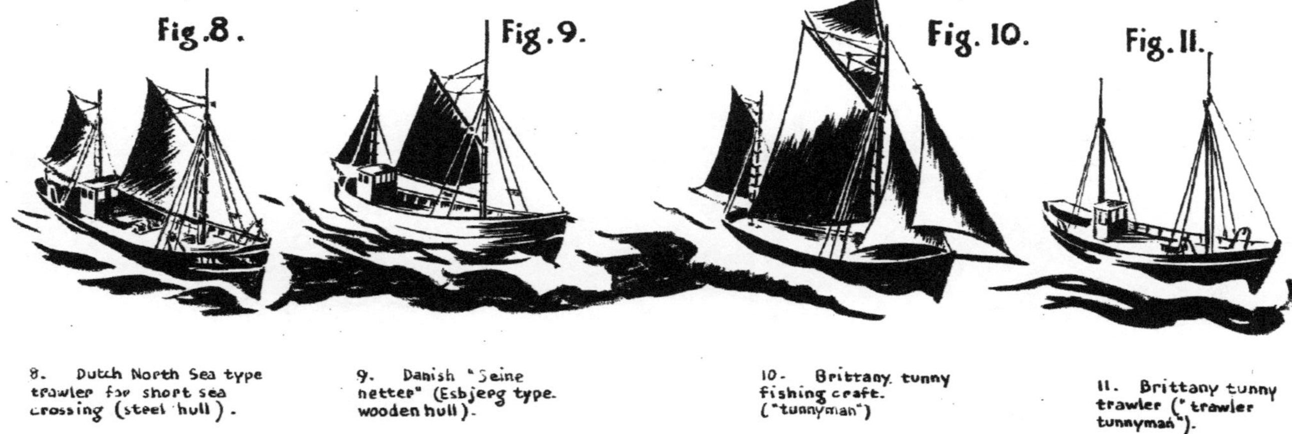

8. Dutch North Sea type trawler for short sea crossing (steel hull).

9. Danish "Seine netter" (Esbjerg type. wooden hull).

10. Brittany tunny fishing craft. ("tunnyman")

11. Brittany tunny trawler ("trawler tunnyman").

Appendix VII.

TRANSPORT OF M.L.Cs..

M.L.Cs. carried on deck, handled by derricks.

M.L.Cs. on large gravity davits.

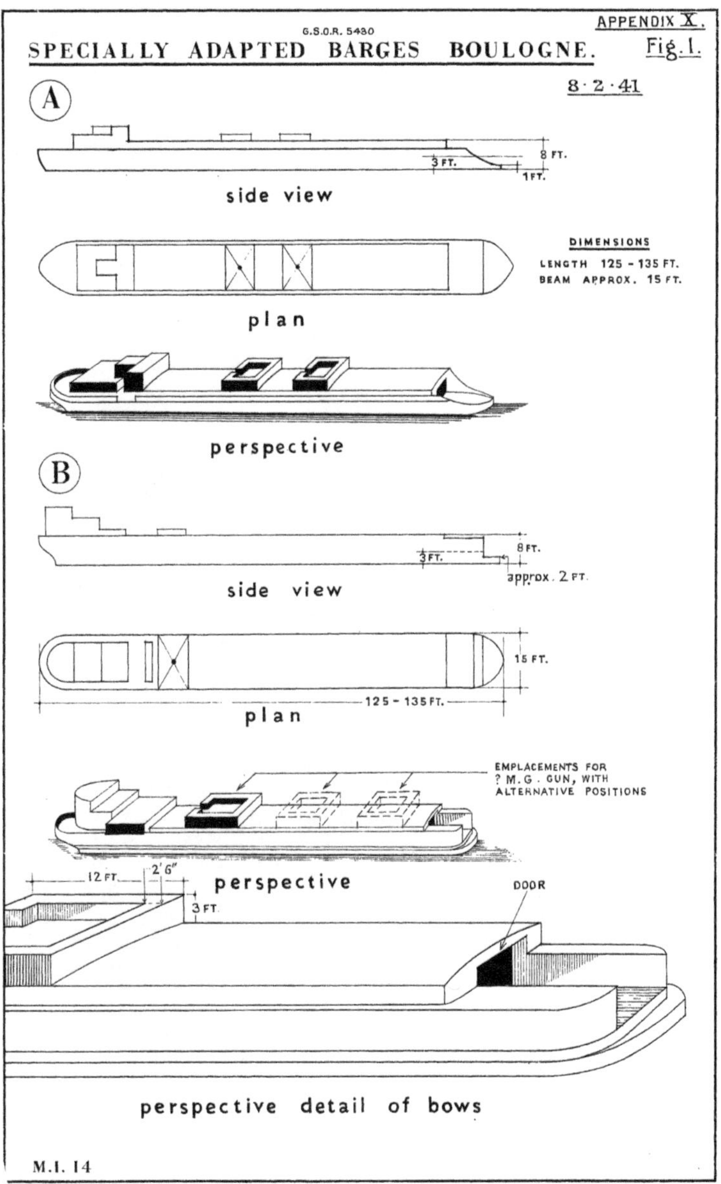

APPENDIX X.
G.S.O.R. 5480
SPECIALLY ADAPTED BARGES BOULOGNE.
Fig. 1.
8·2·41
A
8 FT.
3 FT.
1 FT.
side view
DIMENSIONS
LENGTH 125 - 135 FT.
BEAM APPROX. 15 FT.
plan
perspective
B
8 FT.
3 FT.
approx. 2 FT.
side view
15 FT.
125 - 135 FT.
plan
EMPLACEMENTS FOR
? M.G. GUN, WITH
ALTERNATIVE POSITIONS
perspective
12 FT.
2' 6"
3 FT.
DOOR
perspective detail of bows
M.I. 14

APPENDIX X

Fig. 2

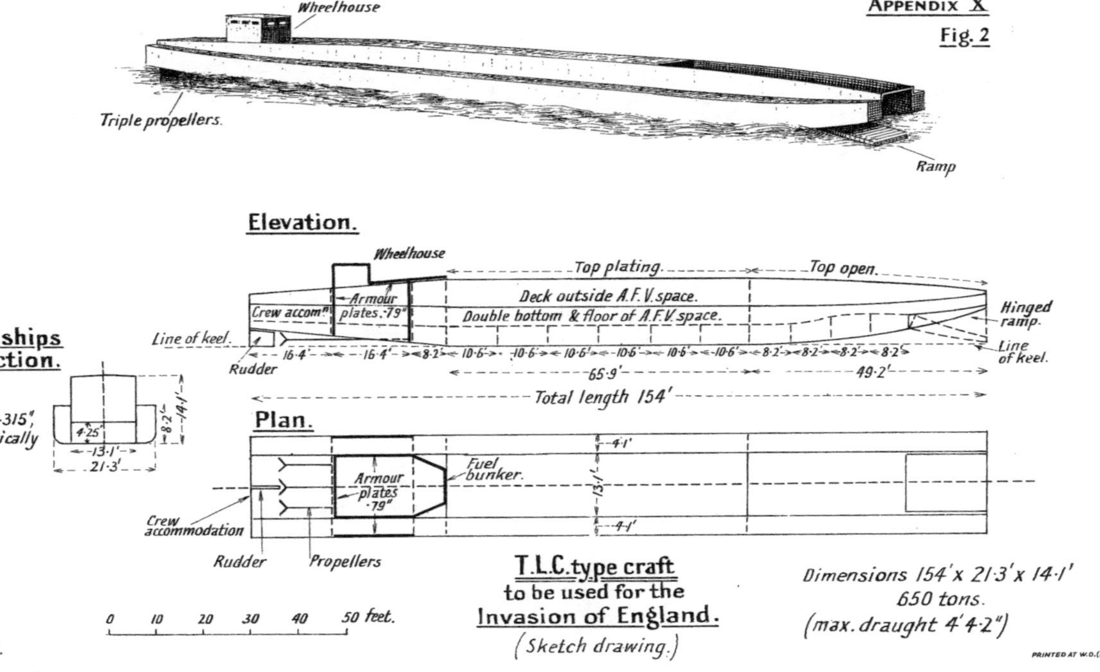
Wheelhouse
Triple propellers.
Ramp
Elevation.
Wheelhouse
Top plating.
Top open.
Armour
plates ·79"
Crew accomⁿ
Deck outside A.F.V. space.
Double bottom & floor of A.F.V. space.
Hinged ramp.
Line of keel.
Line of keel.
Rudder
16·4'
16·4'
8·2'
10·6'
10·6'
10·6'
10·6'
10·6'
10·6'
8·2'
8·2'
8·2'
8·2'
65·9'
49·2'
Total length 154'
Midships section.
Plating ·315", all electrically welded.
4·25"
13·1'
21·3'
8·2'
14·1'
Plan.
4·1'
13·1'
4·1'
Armour plates ·79"
Fuel bunker.
Crew accommodation
Rudder
Propellers
0 10 20 30 40 50 feet.
T.L.C. type craft
to be used for the
Invasion of England.
(Sketch drawing.)
Dimensions 154' x 21·3' x 14·1'
650 tons.
(max. draught 4' 4·2")

M.I.14.

PRINTED AT W.O.(L). 7/41.

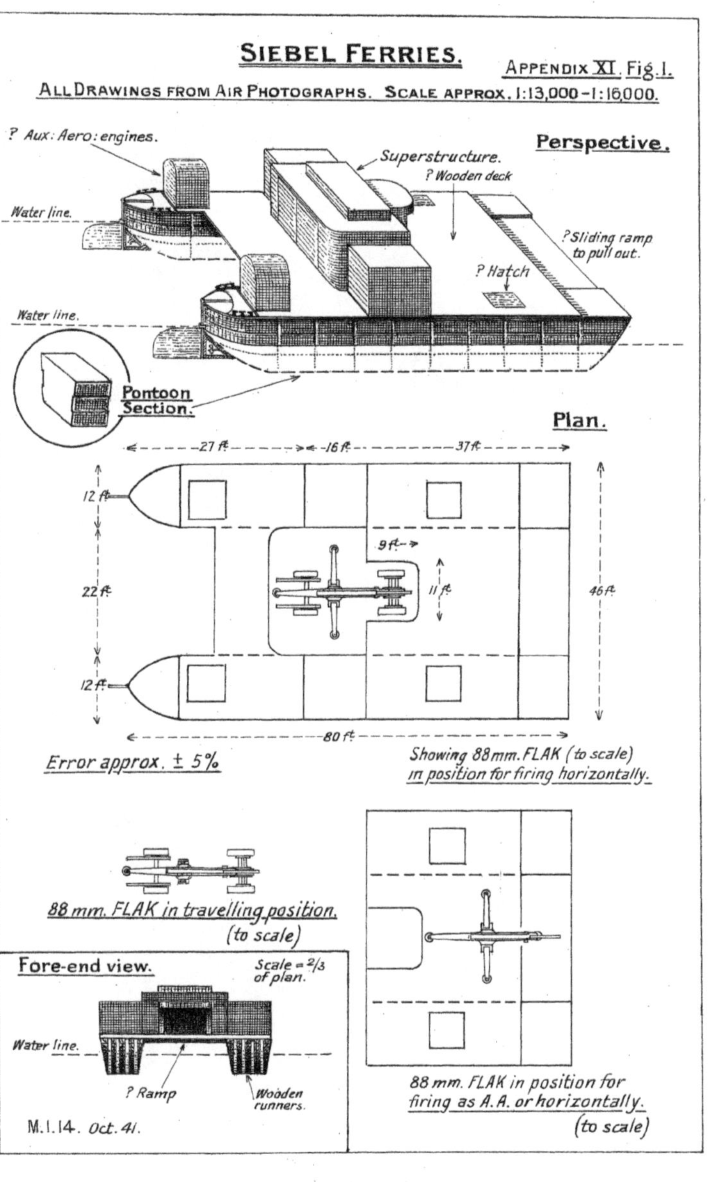
SIEBEL FERRIES.
APPENDIX XI. Fig. I.
ALL DRAWINGS FROM AIR PHOTOGRAPHS. SCALE APPROX. 1:13,000 – 1:16,000.
? Aux: Aero: engines.
Perspective.
Superstructure.
? Wooden deck
Water line.
? Sliding ramp to pull out.
? Hatch
Water line.
Pontoon Section.
Plan.
27 ft
16 ft
37 ft
12 ft
9 ft
22 ft
11 ft
46 ft
12 ft
80 ft
Error approx. ± 5%
Showing 88 mm. FLAK (to scale) in position for firing horizontally.
88 mm. FLAK in travelling position. (to scale)
Fore-end view.
Scale = 2/3 of plan.
Water line.
? Ramp
Wooden runners.
M.I.14. Oct. 41.
88 mm. FLAK in position for firing as A.A. or horizontally. (to scale)

SIEBEL FERRIES.

APPENDIX XI.

SEEN AT CONSTANZA BY GROUND SOURCES.

Fig. 2.

Perspective.

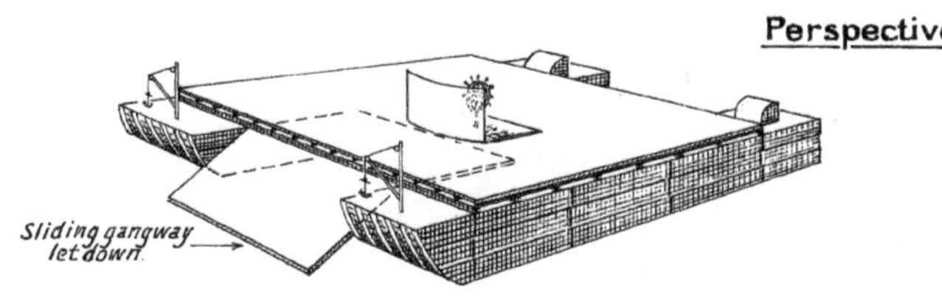

Elevation.

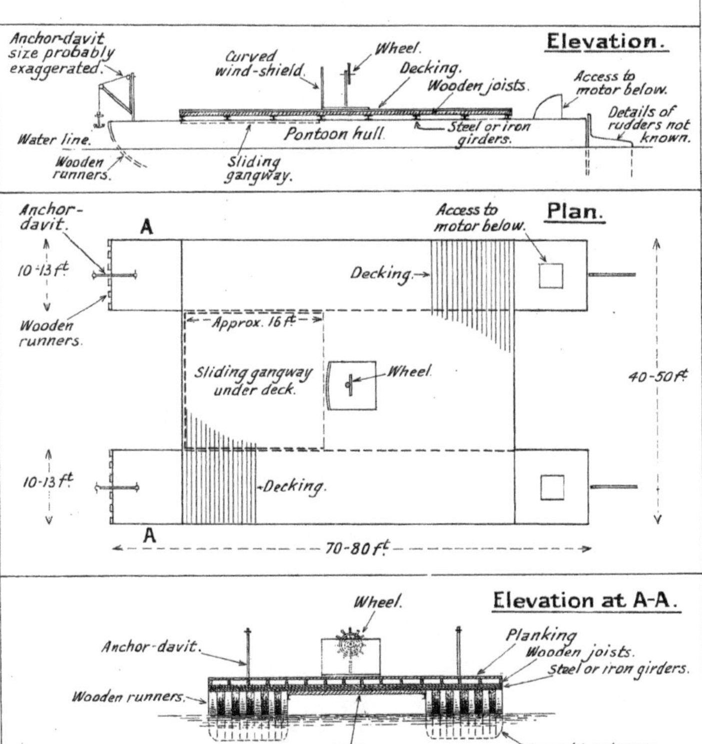

M.I.14. Oct. 1941.

Fig. 3

SECRET

SIEBEL FERRIES,

SEEN Nr STAVANGER, NORWAY.

Based on photograph.

Fig. 4

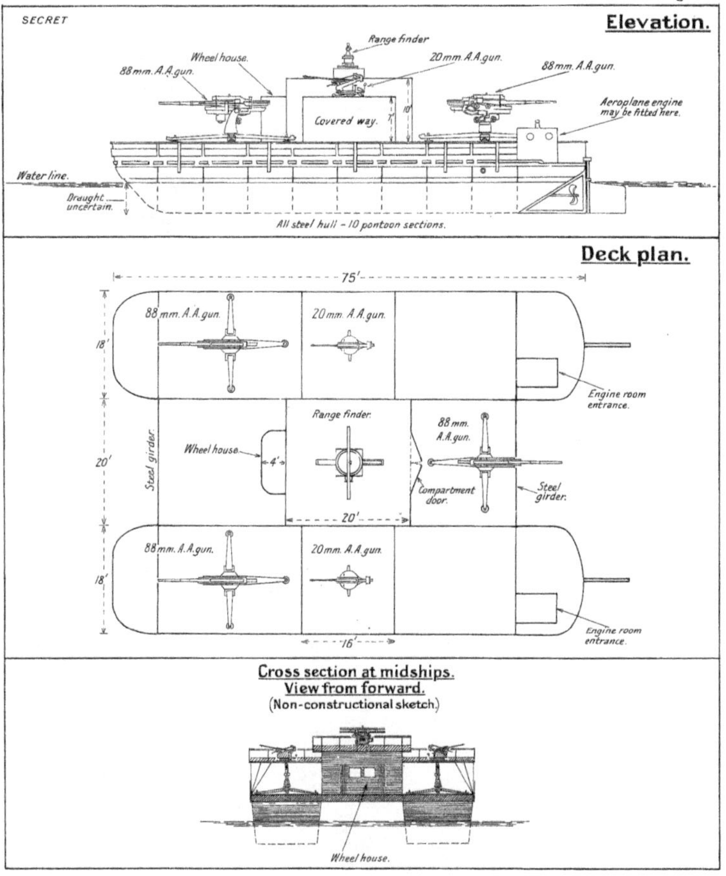
SECRET
Elevation.
Range finder
Wheel house.
20 mm. A.A. gun.
88 mm. A.A. gun.
88 mm. A.A. gun.
Aeroplane engine may be fitted here.
Covered way.
10'
7'
Water line.
Draught uncertain.
All steel hull – 10 pontoon sections.
Deck plan.
75'
88 mm. A.A. gun.
20 mm. A.A. gun.
18'
Engine room entrance.
Range finder.
88 mm. A.A. gun.
Wheel house
4'
Steel girder.
20'
Compartment door.
Steel girder.
20'
88 mm. A.A. gun.
20 mm. A.A. gun.
18'
Engine room entrance.
16'
Cross section at midships.
View from forward.
(Non-constructional sketch.)
Wheel house.

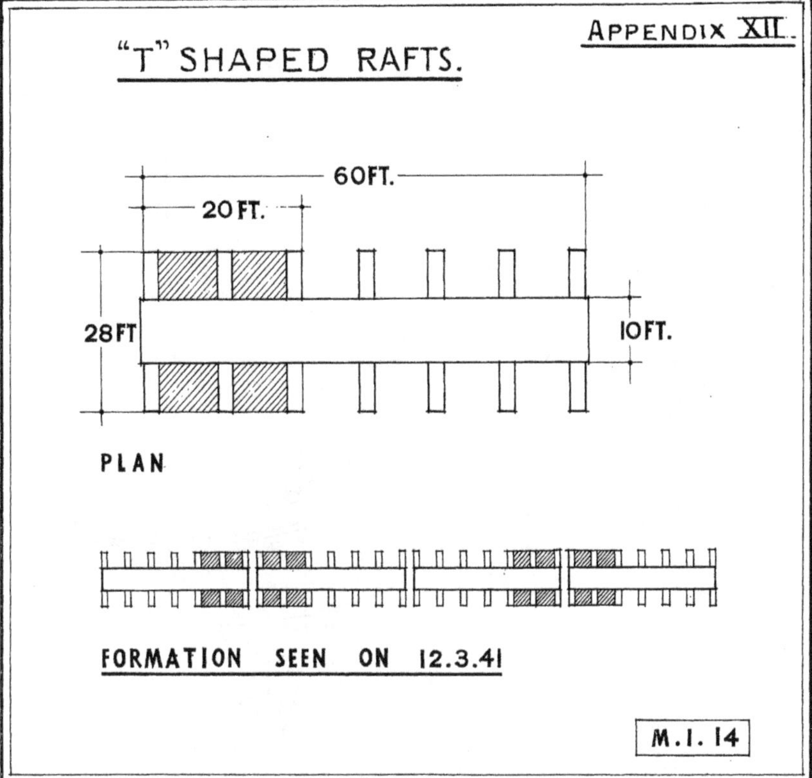
APPENDIX XII.
"T" SHAPED RAFTS.
60FT.
20 FT.
28FT
10FT.
PLAN
FORMATION SEEN ON 12.3.41
M.I. 14

APPENDIX XIX.

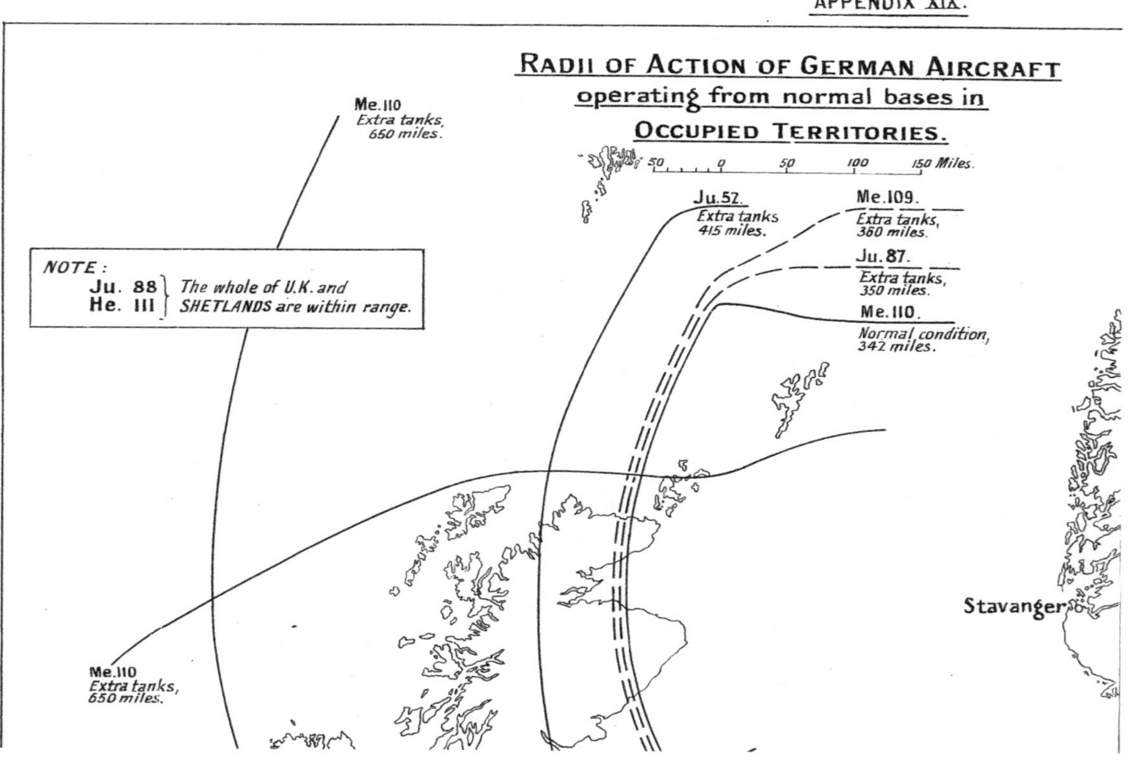

RADII OF ACTION OF GERMAN AIRCRAFT
operating from normal bases in
OCCUPIED TERRITORIES.
50 0 50 100 150 Miles.
Me.110
Extra tanks,
650 miles.
NOTE:
Ju. 88
He. III
The whole of U.K. and
SHETLANDS are within range.
Ju.52.
Extra tanks
415 miles.
Me.109.
Extra tanks,
360 miles.
Ju.87.
Extra tanks,
350 miles.
Me.110.
Normal condition,
342 miles.
Stavanger
Me.110
Extra tanks,
650 miles.

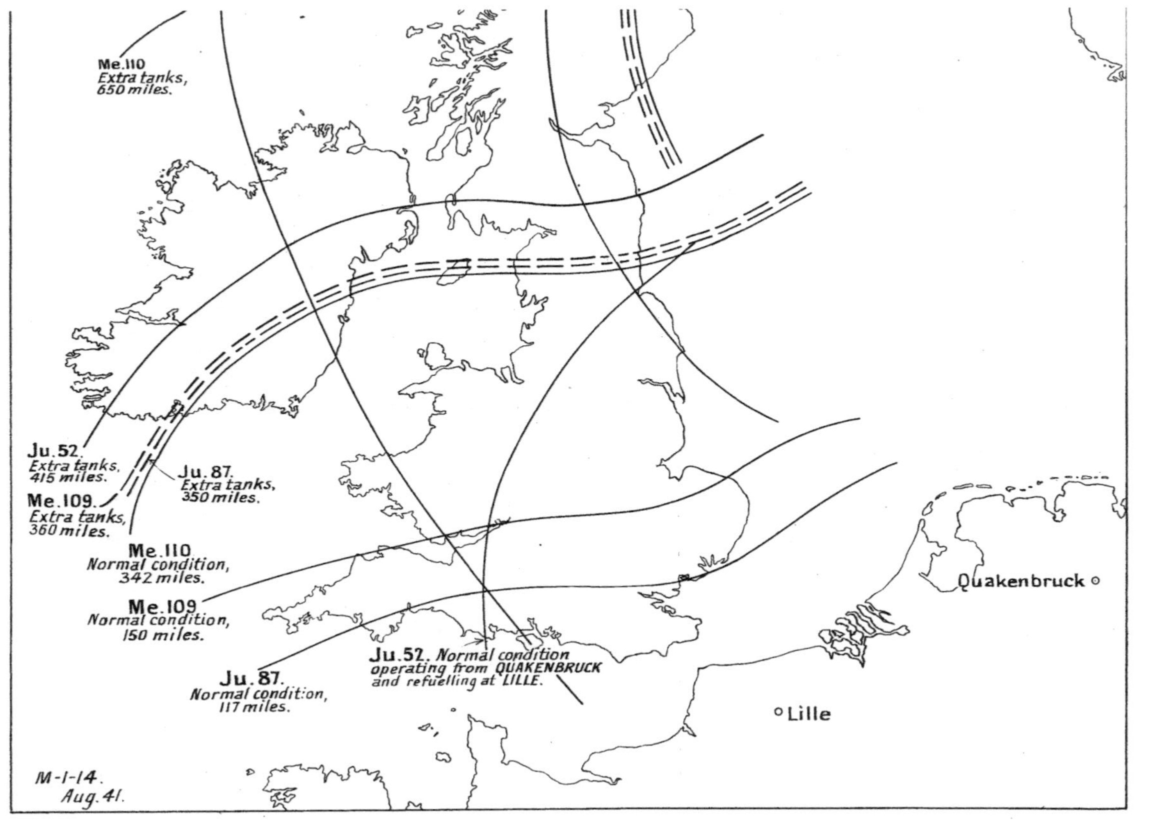
Me.110
Extra tanks,
650 miles.
Ju.52.
Extra tanks,
415 miles.
Ju.87.
Extra tanks,
350 miles.
Me.109.
Extra tanks,
360 miles.
Me.110
Normal condition,
342 miles.
Me.109
Normal condition,
150 miles.
Ju.52. Normal condition
operating from QUAKENBRUCK
and refuelling at LILLE.
Ju.87.
Normal condition,
117 miles.
Quakenbruck
Lille
M-1-14.
Aug. 41.

GERMAN TROOP-CARRYING GLIDER.

APPENDIX XXII.
Fig. I.

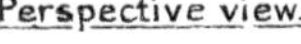

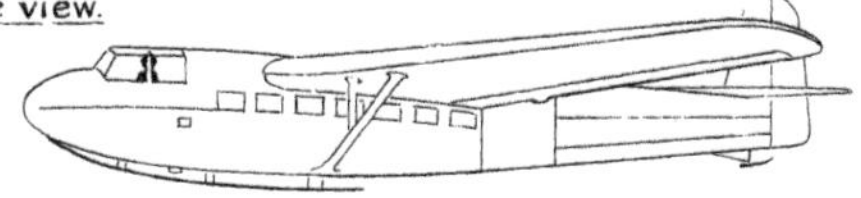

Front view.

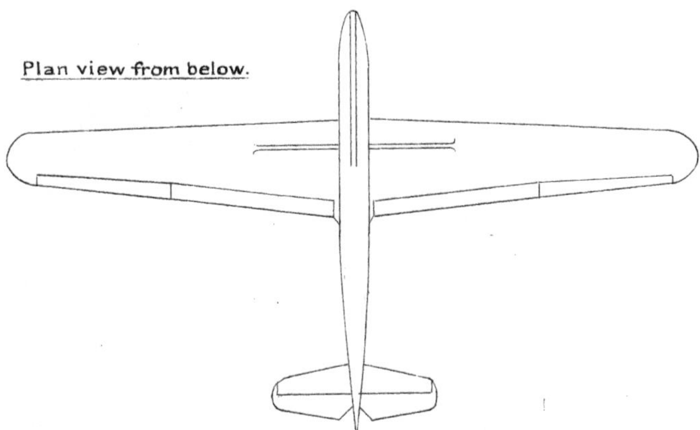

Plan view from below.

Side view.

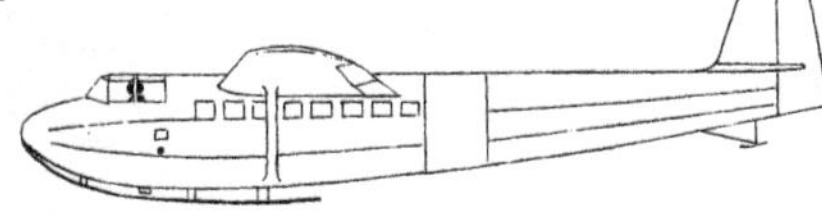

Approx. dimensions.
Span ___ 81' 3"
Length ___ 50 0"
Capacity _ 10 - 12 men.

A. I. Z. (G). No. X/20.
Date 22/2/41.

M-1-14

APPENDIX XXII

GOTHA 242 GLIDER.
(Troop & Freight Transport)

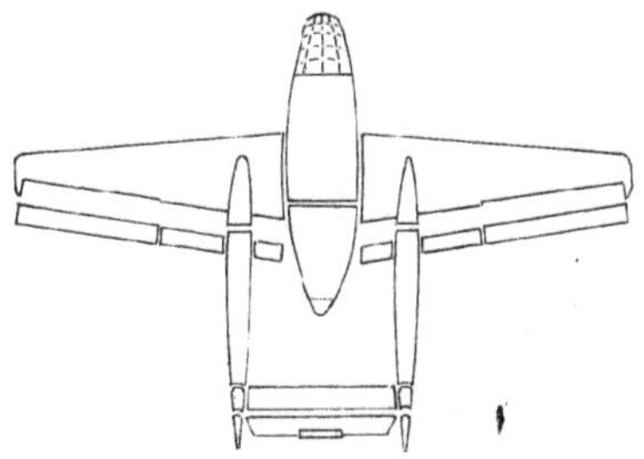

Fig. 1. *Sketch plan (not to scale)*

Fig. 2. *Glider shewing rear of nacelle opened for loading.*

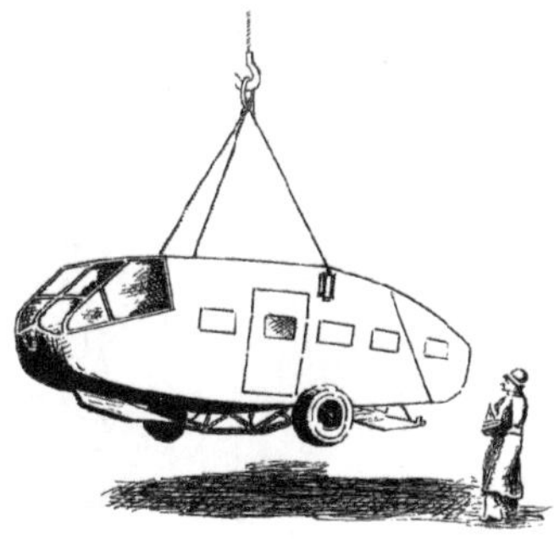

Fig. 3. *Detachable nacelle.*

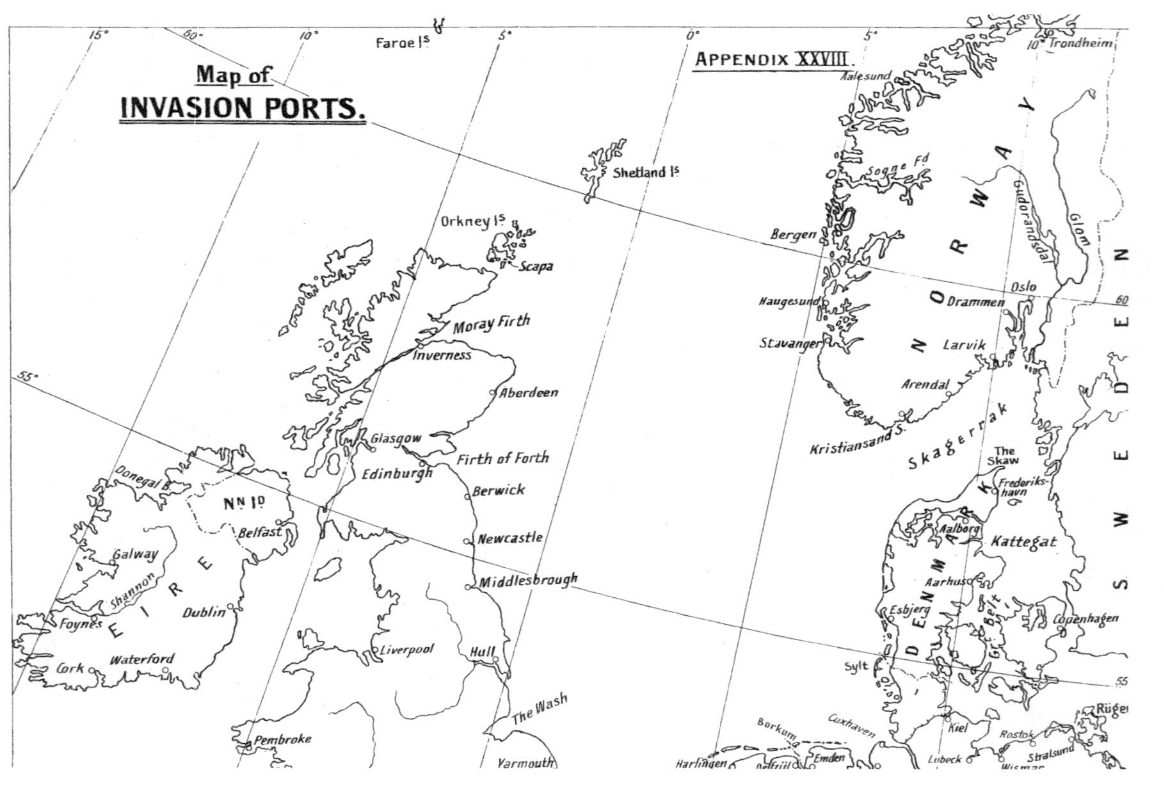
Map of
INVASION PORTS.
APPENDIX XXVIII.
Faroe Is
Shetland Is
Orkney Is
Scapa
Moray Firth
Inverness
Aberdeen
Glasgow
Edinburgh
Firth of Forth
Berwick
Newcastle
Middlesbrough
Hull
Liverpool
The Wash
Yarmouth
Pembroke
Donegal B.
Nn Id
Belfast
Galway
Shannon
EIRE
Dublin
Foynes
Cork
Waterford
NORWAY
Aalesund
Sogne Fd
Bergen
Haugesund
Stavanger
Gudorandsdal
Glom
Oslo
Drammen
Larvik
Arendal
Kristiansand S.
Skagerrak
Trondheim
SWEDEN
The Skaw
Frederikshavn
Aalborg
Kattegat
DENMARK
Aarhus
Esbjerg
Gr. Belt
Copenhagen
Sylt
Kiel
Lubeck
Rostok
Stralsund
Rügen
Borkum
Cuxhaven
Emden
Harlingen
15°
10°
5°
0°
60°
55°
60
55

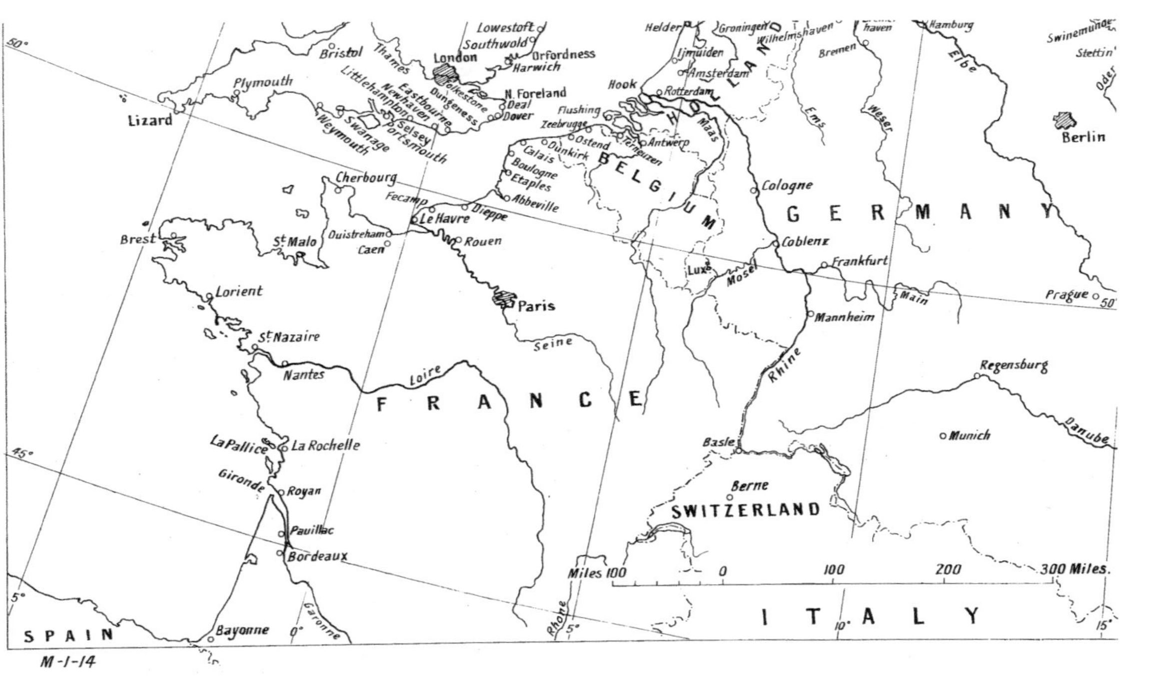

GERMANY
FRANCE
BELGIUM
HOLLAND
SWITZERLAND
ITALY
SPAIN
London
Lowestoft
Southwold
Orfordness
Harwich
N. Foreland
Deal
Dover
Folkestone
Dungeness
Eastbourne
Newhaven
Littlehampton
Selsey
Portsmouth
Swanage
Weymouth
Bristol
Thames
Plymouth
Lizard
Helder
Ijmuiden
Amsterdam
Hook
Rotterdam
Groningen
Wilhelmshaven
Bremen
Hamburg
Swinemunde
Stettin
Oder
Elbe
Weser
Ems
Berlin
Flushing
Zeebrugge
Ostend
Terneuzen
Antwerp
Maas
Dunkirk
Calais
Boulogne
Etaples
Abbeville
Cherbourg
Fecamp
Dieppe
Le Havre
Rouen
Ouistreham
Caen
St. Malo
Brest
Lorient
St. Nazaire
Nantes
Loire
Paris
Seine
La Pallice
La Rochelle
Gironde
Royan
Pauillac
Bordeaux
Garonne
Bayonne
Cologne
Coblenz
Frankfurt
Main
Mannheim
Lux.
Mosel
Rhine
Prague
Regensburg
Munich
Danube
Basle
Berne
Rhone
Miles 100
0
100
200
300 Miles.
50°
45°
5°
0°
5°
10°
15°
50°
M-1-14

www.ingramcontent.com/pod-product-compliance
Lightning Source LLC
Chambersburg PA
CBHW030934150426
42812CB00064B/2844/J
* 9 7 8 1 8 4 7 3 4 3 7 6 5 *